A CHILD NO MORE

A CHILD NO MORE

Mary Pytches

HODDER AND STOUGHTON
LONDON   SYDNEY   AUCKLAND

All Biblical quotations are taken from the New International Version unless otherwise stated in the text.

British Library Cataloguing in Publication Data
Pytches, Mary
  A child no more.
  1. Adults. Psychological development – Christian viewpoints
  I. Title
  261.515
  ISBN 0-340-54998-X

Published by Hodder and Stoughton, a division of Hodder and Stoughton Ltd, Mill Road, Dunton Green, Sevenoaks, Kent TN13 2YA. Editorial Office: 47 Bedford Square, London WC1B 3DP.
Photoset by Medcalf Type Ltd, Bicester, Oxon.
Printed in Great Britain by Cox & Wyman Ltd, Reading.

To my friend and co-worker,
Prue Bedwell,
whose loyalty, patience and loving support
have been invaluable in my own spiritual pilgrimage,
and also in our many travels around the world.

CONTENTS

INTRODUCTION

For many years now I have been involved with Christians who desire to make changes in their lives. The request for help may have been prompted by a variety of reasons: difficult feelings, such as anger or depression, which are interfering with everyday life; self-destructive attitudes which threaten growth, or even survival; or unhealthy behaviour patterns which have proved hard to correct. In some cases the problem may be affecting not only the individual persons concerned, but also those with whom they live.

During the course of counselling and prayer with such people I have noticed certain factors which, when present, give hope that some real progress is possible. I refer to these as disciplines for growth. If they have been neglected, very little headway has been achieved, but when practised, appropriate, and even profound, changes have occurred.

I must explain that I am not a professional counsellor and therefore I have no experience of working with the mentally sick. My rôle has been as a prayer counsellor in a local church situation. In a church, pastoral caring may take many different forms. Prayerful, loving support may be offered to any person suffering from a mental illness. However, it is not advisable to offer prayer counselling to someone in the process of a psychotic breakdown. This sort of person will be out of touch with reality and have no capacity to be insightful about himself. If we suspect a severe neurosis or mental disturbance we would immediately recommend such a person to seek professional help.

In listing the disciplines required for growth, I am speaking to those who are in the fortunate position of having the mental health and strength to make changes. This is not to deny they have suffered emotional damage and may be sensing considerable inner pain, but, as far as any of us can be termed 'normal', these are normal people with the ability to face reality about themselves and those around them.

In my book *Yesterday's Child* I attempted to look at ways by which childhood traumas may be healed. This book, *A Child No More*, points us forwards to maturity. It is not too difficult to diagnose a problem or uncover its root cause, but overcoming it in the present is frequently an uphill struggle. In my view the following disciplines are vital to this process.

Change is fundamental to the Christian life. A continual transformation should be taking place within each of us as a normal maturation process. Adherence to these disciplines will not only advance this process but should facilitate the removal of any blockages to this growth occurring.

A Child No More is about God's marvellous plan for us to be transformed into the likeness of Jesus. 'For those God foreknew he also predestined to be conformed to the likeness of his Son, that he might be the firstborn among many brothers' (Rom.8:29). Although it is God's purpose to have a family which is growing up and becoming like their 'older brother' Jesus, too many of us settle for far less than this. Different things hinder our growth, and too often we are tempted to think we have gone as far as we can. The writer to the Hebrews tells us to 'throw off everything that hinders and the sin that so easily entangles' and to 'run with perseverance the race marked out for us' (Heb.12:1).

Lest we fall into the trap of thinking we can earn our salvation through our own efforts, we must remind ourselves that we are saved by grace (Eph.2:8,9). It is also true that our present position before God is that 'we have been made holy' (Heb.10:10). Nevertheless we are also told to ' "be holy, because I am holy" ' (1 Pet.1:16).

It is plain, therefore, that on the one hand we are already holy in Christ and on the other we must continue to work out our salvation by following after holiness. Yet even the work of becoming holy is impossible on our own. Ultimately this transformation 'comes from the Lord, who is the Spirit' (2 Cor.3:18). Apart from Him we can do nothing (John 15:5). However, God chooses to involve us in the process and demands our full co-operation. Paul told us to work out our salvation 'with fear and trembling' (Phil.2:12). The root of the word translated 'salvation' comes from the Greek *sozo*, which may also imply 'wholeness'. So it could read: 'continue to work out your "wholeness" with fear and trembling, for it is God who works in you to will and to act according to his good purpose' (Phil.2:12,13).

This work may sometimes be hard and would be impossible without assistance from many different sources. The grace of God is, of course, our primary source of help. Then there are friends who come alongside us with encouragement and wise counsel. Besides all this, a very significant element in my own growth process has been learning to utilise the disciplines it is the purpose of this book to outline. Without them I could have achieved very little actual change.

I have used the story of the prodigal son as the ground plan for this book. The different steps in his journey back to his father denote the variety of disciplines we all need to employ if we want to become mature. The different steps are all to be found in the Gospel, although I have taken liberties in expanding it a little more graphically!

This is not a book to be read at one sitting! It will be of greater benefit and more easily digested if it is tackled a chapter at a time. At the conclusion of each chapter there are some exercises which can be worked at alone or with others. If you are in a group which is larger than three or four, it would be better to break into smaller groups to do the exercises after reading the chapter together. Because of the intimacy and trust which is implicit in sharing at such a personal level it would be best to keep to the same group for each session. Whether the book is used with friends, or alone, it would be good to keep a journal in which to note the exercises. This would also serve to log progress and for starting or maintaining a dialogue with God. In it you can relate your struggles and longings and then give Him the time and opportunity to respond. As the Lord begins to speak to the inner ear, it would be good to write down what you believe He may be saying. Practising His presence in this way will be the most beneficial of all the disciplines.

As always I owe a debt of gratitude to my husband, David, who patiently reads my manuscripts with his critical eye. I am indebted to Liz Heike and Richard Bedwell for giving me such positive help and criticism. I have used many examples from the lives of those I have met at meetings or counselled over the years. These I have disguised in such a way that the people are unrecognisable, although otherwise the experiences remain factual. Some, however, have given me permission to use their story without a disguise, for which I am grateful.

The causes of immaturity are often easy to find. Discovering a way through them is the harder part. My prayer and desire is that this book will effectively help those who are truly seeking to be changed into the likeness of Jesus.

1. SURVIVAL vs WHOLENESS

'Slowly and compulsively the false self closes its
hard, brittle shell around us, and our loneliness
remains.'[1]

A young girl sat nervously in our sitting-room. I knew what
she wanted to say before she spoke. For months I had
watched her growing discomfort in church. In 1981 the Holy
Spirit began a new and powerful work in our fellowship.
Some people loved it and welcomed it, but others, like our
visitor, were uncomfortable and wished the services would
return to being safe and predictable. Jean explained that
every time God began to move in power among the people
she would leave the church in a hurry. She said that she felt
as if she was going to choke, and just had to escape. Now
that she had had time to watch people's lives and see the
changes in them, she was convinced that it had been God
at work after all and she wanted to be a part of it. She
recognised that it was fear which stopped her. She explained
that this same crippling fear blocked her in other areas of
her life also, but she had no idea what it was due to or how
to overcome it.

I asked her if she was ready to look for the root cause
and deal with it. She seemed to become anxious and was
silent for some time. Eventually she hung her head and told
me she didn't think she was yet. 'That's OK,' I said. 'You
just let me know when you are ready and then we will spend
some time together and see what God has to show us.' After

this she left and for another whole year continued to make rapid exits from church. She was protecting herself and by doing so was preventing her own healing and growth.

The objective of wholeness

Jesus told His followers that they were to 'Be perfect . . . as your heavenly Father is perfect' (Matt.5:48). The word 'perfect' can be used to convey the idea of goodness, but it can also mean 'complete' or 'made whole'. Wholeness and maturity are part of the purpose and plan of God for every Christian. Therefore, to stop growing or to reject growth for any reason is not only depressing but is contrary to God's purpose. Why then are so many people avoiding the process of 'being completed'?

One reason may be that a person is unaware that his life has become static. He believes his experience is the norm for a Christian. Possibly he acknowledges the lack of progress, but feels himself powerless to change. Yet another reason could be that, like Jean, he has chosen to play it safe. He does not want to rock the boat. I am happy to say that Jean did eventually come back for help. It was the beginning of an incredible work of healing that God did in her life.

Sitting and listening to people's problems and attempting to understand what has caused their present difficulty, I have become increasingly aware of what I would term their 'survival kits'. These are defence mechanisms which serve to protect or defend the inner-self from being further hurt. These 'kits', constructed and fashioned over the years, are the real problems so many people are having to grapple with. They will block a person's growth indefinitely unless the difficult work of laying them down is accomplished.

By trying to clarify the complex workings of a human personality there is a danger of becoming too simplistic and leaving the picture still incomplete. Nevertheless, it is worth the risk if it succeeds in helping some people to find a way through the impasse in their lives.

The hurts to our inner-self

We all share the common experience of being born into a hurting, imperfect world as tiny, dependent babies, each with an inbuilt bias towards sin. Nevertheless, our inherited family characteristics and tendencies, our individual physical features and personalities make us, each one, into totally unique people.

With the best will in the world it is impossible to protect a child against the disappointments and frustrations of life. So it will not be long before a new baby becomes subjected to pain. He may quite soon experience what, to his immature emotions, appears to be major rejection, when he is left to cry for a longer time than feels bearable. His mother may be unable to express love in a tactile way and the baby is starved of that necessary touching. He may feel abused by an over-tired and depressed parent. He may have to endure hunger at the hands of an immature parent. One way or another, this little baby will suffer the pain of totally unmet, or only partially met, needs. He may even be the recipient of appalling injuries at the hands of a violent parent. Suffering, then, soon becomes part of any child's normal experience of life and the emerging-self may be damaged by this. After describing a dysfunctional family to a group of a hundred people, I asked those who felt that their family of origin fitted my description to raise their hands. About 80% did. Despite this they appeared, at least on the surface, to be quite normal people. How did they survive the pain of their dysfunctional family background?

'Survival kits'

Every human being is born with a powerful instinct for survival. Come what may he will try to endure – somehow! He may have to die inside a little in the process. He may have to construct some strong walls to defend and protect the damaged inner-self. He may have to fashion an acceptable false outer-self. But sooner or later, whatever line of defence is chosen, his 'survival kit' will be erected and put to good use. This mechanism is in fact a man's natural response to pain. It does the job of protecting against further hurt or easing present hurt. It will involve both defensive as well as offensive elements. It will probably evolve subtle tactics, and possibly some less subtle ones, for getting a back-log of the unmet needs satisfied. The objective is the minimising of inner pain. It is a fabrication of emotional, rational and behavioural responses to cope with internal discomfort.

In her book *An Aspect of Fear*, Grace Sheppard, the wife of the Bishop of Liverpool, describes this 'survival kit': 'Loss can hurt, so we build defences, to cushion ourselves against a sudden assault on our senses, our bodies or on the lives of those close to us. We fear losing little bits of our life and try to defend ourselves against being hurt. Instead of putting our energies into living, we concentrate on surviving and develop a siege mentality, expecting trouble.'[2]

In his fascinating novel, *The Power of One*, Bryce Courtenay tells the story of Peekay, an English-speaking boy, born and brought up in South Africa. At the age of five he is sent away from his adored black nanny to a brutal, Dickensian-type boarding school. Not only is he the youngest boy in the school by two years, but also the only English-speaking one. Somehow he manages to endure the brutal treatment of the other children, who are led by the master bully they nickname 'the Judge'. He only manages to endure this by erecting a 'survival kit'.

Towards the end of the book and grown-up at last, Peekay

reflects on this defence mechanism, or what he calls his 'camouflage', or an 'outer skin'.

> I had become an expert at camouflage . . . I had come to identify with my camouflage to the point where the masquerade had become more important than the truth. While this posturing was so finely tuned it was no longer deliberate, it had nevertheless been born out of a compulsion to hide . . . My camouflage, begun so many years before under the persecution of the 'Judge', was now threatening to become the complete man. It was time to slough the mottled and cunningly contrived outer skin and emerge as myself, to face the risk of exposure, to regain the power of one. I had reached the point where to find myself was essential.'[3]

As we have seen, this process of erecting a 'survival kit' can start at a very tender age and may continue on throughout life. Yesterday I saw a young girl whose reaction to childhood hurt was a clinging dependency upon others. Her inner-child only seemed to stop hurting when she was attached to someone stronger who would care for her. That was her 'camouflage'.

At the other extreme I was talking to a woman who refuses to need other people. She would rather live in independent isolation than have to trust anyone. To depend upon other human beings, she fears, would cause unnecessary suffering for her. 'They will not be there when I need them.' 'They will be unreliable.' 'They will let me down.' These are the messages she uses to control her inner needs. To be let down would only re-activate the pain within her fragmented heart. She protects herself by never putting herself in the position of being hurt again. Anger towards anyone who attempts to get close to her is part of her 'survival kit'. As a result she has become a lonely and isolated person. This defence mechanism has been there for a long time; it has become an habitual life pattern and appears, to her mind, quite rational. After all, no child having burnt his fingers once will voluntarily put his hand in the fire again.

Our two-year-old grandson, Zachary, proved this the other morning when he came down to breakfast and refused to sit up at the table while the hot-water-bottle was lying on it. The night before he had seen it for the first time when it was hot. Curious, he had tried to touch it and had suffered the consequences. Now, having learned his painful lesson, he refused to go near it. He was not going to take any more risks even though we assured him that it was now quite cold.

Zachary will, no doubt, get over that one brief episode with the hot-water-bottle. However, a child who has suffered recurring pain throughout his childhood will not easily give up his carefully constructed 'survival kit' even when he is an adult and no longer needs it. The incest victim who has been raped regularly by a relative over a long period will have found a way to survive such horrific treatment. This protective mechanism could remain locked in place for the rest of her life unless some help is sought which will enable her to dismantle and discard it.

Anyone from a dysfunctional family background where there was poor communication, parental absenteeism and interruptions of the love process, suffers major hurt. Over the years he will have adapted to his environment and discovered his own way of survival. On the other hand, a child from a secure home, where communication was good and the parents were present for him, both emotionally and physically, will have received enough love along the way to heal most of his hurts and to keep his inner-self intact. He will have learned how to discharge pain in a healthy way at the time it was felt and healing will have occurred naturally and spontaneously. It is the build-up of unexpressed pain that necessitates the construction of a 'survival kit'.

An adult from a secure background is still vulnerable to

the whole range of human feelings, including painful ones, and may still need to protect himself in some areas of his life. Generally, however, his hurt is not met by a protective barrier, instead it goes straight to the heart and is discharged through tears or talking about it in a healthy way. The real-self is allowed to show. There is no pretence, no 'camouflage', no 'survival kit' because none is needed.

As we have seen, everyone creates his own unique 'survival kit' in response to his particular inner pain. These individual reactions are also influenced and reinforced by his inherited characteristics and his fallen nature. They are a human way of handling life's hurts apart from God. They spring from the flesh and are therefore basically sinful. As Richard Lovelace writes,

> Sin cannot be limited to isolated instances or patterns of wrongdoing; it is something much more akin to the psychological term 'complex': an organic network of compulsive attitudes, beliefs and behaviour deeply rooted in our alienation from God.[4]

The struggle to change

This way-of-being may continue unchallenged until the person becomes a Christian. Then the struggle to change begins. One new Christian repents of his angry outbursts and seeks to control them. Another recognises that sexual promiscuity is no longer for him and, repenting, determines to overcome the temptation.

The first problem for the Christian is to decide what things in his life actually need to be put to death and then how it is to be done. Some practices and habits are quite obviously sinful, but others appear neither specifically sinful nor yet particularly godly; kind of neutral. What often happens is that the bad is controlled by suppression whilst the apparently harmless is retained but Christianised and made to appear godly. Richard Lovelace brings focus to bear on this when he writes: 'Most congregations of professing Christians today are saturated with a kind of "dead goodness", an ethical respectability which has its motivational roots in the flesh rather than in the illuminating and enlivening control of the Holy Spirit.'[5]

Susan's experience is quite common. As a young child she had received very little affection from her mother and had felt rejected by her. This had left her with deep longings for love and acceptance, especially from the female sex. On becoming a Christian she had suppressed her attraction for the same sex and refused to give way to a lesbian life-style. Her reactions to the bad inner feelings of being unacceptable changed very little, however. She had always worked hard to win approval and be liked. Now she won approval by helping and caring for others. This served to minimise the inner pain of feeling unacceptable. The original inner hurt had not been healed so she continued to need and use a 'survival kit'. The most unacceptable part of which had gone underground, whilst the more acceptable part had stayed, although with a slightly different name-tag. The new 'tag' did not, however, alter its fleshly roots. One of the problems with merely suppressing the bad and ungodly part is the tendency it then has to surface unexpectedly. Occasionally Susan would find herself strongly attracted to someone of the same sex. Feelings of love, jealousy, possessiveness and hurt would then beset the relationship and Susan would spiral into guilt and depression.

Putting the 'survival kit' down

What we need to realise is that a 'survival kit' is a carnal structure erected with the sole purpose of keeping the damaged inner-self from feeling too much pain. The flesh, with all its crafty and deceitful ways, must be put to death. The whole kit has to be dismantled and given up. 'Everything that does not come from faith is sin' (Rom.14:23). Defence mechanisms do not come from faith. They are there in reaction to pain, fear and unbelief. However, they are difficult to put down whilst the pain is so acute. Once the hurt has abated a little there is a decreasing need for protection. When this occurs a 'survival kit' is no longer needed and the individual can choose to lay down the now outdated defence mechanisms and start on the road to wholeness.

In his book, *The Great Divorce*, C.S. Lewis tells the story of a dream bus journey to 'the Valley of the Shadow of Life'. A place that could become Heaven if the right choice was made. Whilst there he watches an encounter between an Angel and a Ghost carrying a red Lizard on his shoulder. The Lizard constantly whispers in the Ghost's ear, tempting him with unclean thoughts. The Ghost is reticent about killing the Lizard, although the Angel offers to do it for him if the Ghost will just give him permission. The Lizard pleads to remain, painting a picture of what life would be like for the Ghost without him. Only after a great struggle does the Ghost finally consent and the Angel kills the Lizard. As he does so the Ghost reels backwards from the pain of the killing, but immediately a transformation starts and the Ghost begins to change into a heavenly man. First comes the arm and the shoulder, then, brighter still and stronger, the legs and hands. The neck and golden head materialised whilst he watched and if his attention had not wavered he would have seen the actual completing of an immense, golden man who was not much smaller than the Angel. At the same time the dead Lizard is also transformed into a magnificent white stallion. Lewis then asks his Teacher if he is right in thinking the Lizard really turned into the Horse. 'Aye, but it was killed first. Ye'll not forget that part of the story?' replies the Teacher.[6]

Other encounters between Angels and Ghosts do not have such happy endings. The book is a story of choices. A choice between hanging on to some out-dated mode of behaviour which keeps people chained to Hell or of letting it go, denying it and experiencing the transformation which prepares them for Heaven.

The work of healing and change

The journey through to wholeness is often difficult and painful. No one dismantles his 'survival kit' without protest. Most frequently a person will come to a point of recognising that things in his life are not right and he begins to cry out to God for help. He may also seek help from a counsellor. God hears his prayer and begins to penetrate, by His Spirit, through the protective layers into the inner pain. As He does this the protective 'survival kit' starts to disintegrate. However, God will not take it away. Only the individual person can decide to lay it down. God waits for us to recognise this 'kit' as a fabrication of the flesh and therefore something to be repented of. He waits to see if we really are sorry for our ungodly habits and sinful ways of getting our needs met. Only then will He help us by the power of His indwelling Spirit in the changes that need to be made.

We recently counselled Sara, a woman who had experienced much unhappiness in her childhood. She had made some poor choices in her adult life and her present circumstances were very difficult as a result. She had been imploring God to help her change. As we talked, the Holy Spirit began to give the insight into the wrong reactions she had had to her parents' inept handling of her as a child. These reactions had distorted the way she thought and felt as well as affecting her behaviour. She began to weep in sorrow. As we prayed she cried out again and again, 'Please

God forgive me.' Her repentance was strong and real and she was able to receive God's forgiveness. Then we prayed for Jesus to come and heal her. As together we waited on God the Holy Spirit gave her a clear picture of herself in a filthy room in which there was a bed crawling with insects. Sara said she felt very small and although she saw a bucket and mop there she did not feel able to clean the room alone. We continued to wait on God. We were amazed at His words to her. She said that she became aware of Jesus in the next room and when she looked to Him for help, He spoke these words to her: 'Some things I will do for you; some things we will do together and some things you will have to do on your own while I watch.'

Sara had heard the truth. Only she could do the repenting necessary and set about 'putting off' her 'survival kit'. God could not do that for her. Only He could forgive and heal her; she could not do that for herself. But only in co-operation with God would she be able to change her behaviour patterns. This work of change is the time-consuming part.

We often meet people who testify to amazing healing encounters with Jesus through the inner healing ministry. It is then disappointing to learn that the healing appeared to last only a short time. The failure, I believe, is due to misconceptions about this ministry. For many the relief from pain has been the objective. For others the removal of an inconvenient problem has been their goal. We forget that God's aim for us is maturity, wholeness and Christ-likeness. When we are involved in this ongoing process the occasional inner-healing experience becomes a part of it.

God loves to heal us and He loves to help us with our problems in the same way as an earthly father loves to comfort his children when they are in pain. It is all part and parcel of fatherhood. But more than anything a father's heart-desire is to see his child grow and mature. Time and energy will be needed for God's children to reach this objective. Healing will have an important place, but so too will repentance and change. Perseverance will be needed until the new behaviour feels as comfortable and fitting as the old 'survival kit'.

The work to be done by each of us is simple to understand, but not so simple to effect. For some very damaged people this whole operation may take years of blood, toil, tears and sweat but the on-going process will bring blessing. A healed homosexual recently said it had taken him six years to become whole in that area of his life. It had been a long painful road and he had had to learn and use many different disciplines before the change was accomplished.

You may be starting from square one with none or little insight into your own 'survival kits'. Whether you start from the beginning or part way down the road to healing the following chapters could become a useful tool to help you reach a greater degree of wholeness. It is my prayer that they will.

Exercises

These can be done in a small group or with a friend. Remember that trust and confidence takes time to develop. Share only as much as you feel able to with your group. If the exercises are done alone, use a journal and share your findings directly with God.

First read the chapter together.

1. Sit quietly for five minutes and each visualise yourself at the age of six. Then picture your childhood home. Take up your place in the room most used by the family. First see your father enter the room; take time to let your reactions to him register. Then see your mother come in and note your feelings towards her.

Now share these reactions with your group.

2. Did you need to use any form of 'survival' during your childhood?

3. Is this 'survival kit' still in operation in your life? If so what form does it take?

4. Is your 'survival kit' meeting a need or is it protecting you from something? Using the words of Psalm 139, verses 23 and 24, ask God to show you the truth.

Any habitual technique for handling discomfort will take time to lay down. You may need to start by allowing Jesus to heal any residue of inner pain your defence mechanism may be protecting.

5. Take time to pray for any member of the group who has begun to get in touch with some discomfort. Begin by inviting Jesus to come and heal. Give Him time to minister to each individual. Do not intrude with good ideas, just quietly bless what He is doing.

Remember, expressing grief can be part of the healing and releasing forgiveness to those who caused the hurt is an important part of the resolution.

2. THE MEANING OF DISCIPLINE

'Let us be among those who believe that the inner transformation of our lives is worth our best effort.'[1]

In the previous chapter we have seen that the complex 'survival kit' some people erect in order to protect their hurting inner-self is to be our main focus of concern. These 'kits' act as barriers, preventing the inner-self not only from being hurt again but from being even seen or heard. Consequently there is not much chance of healing whilst this defence mechanism remains in place. This 'kit' very often becomes a false-self hiding the truth about the real-self. It is like a lie which covers up the truth. Thus, anger is shown instead of hurt, blame instead of shame, jealousy instead of need. To drop the lie and to have the inner-self healed of its hurt, shame and painful needs will take time and discipline.

The meaning of discipline

Discipline can be understood to mean punishment or chastisement; something to be suffered as a consequence of some mistake or wrong-doing. For instance, on a different level, even the discipline of dieting could be seen as a punishment for over-eating. But discipline does not have to be something punitive. The word can also be used to mean 'self-control'. One dictionary definition is 'to train or to bring under control'. The discipline of dieting can then be seen in the positive light of helping the body towards better health.

Disciplines can serve rather like rails that steer a tram safely through a built-up city, preventing it from veering to left or right. Recently I bought a small clockwork train for my visiting grandsons to play with. When two-year-old Philip arrives he can never wait for the tracks to be laid out for him, so he will play with the train without the tracks. It struggles drunkenly across the floor bumping into everything in its way, frequently falling over on its back, all wheels a-whirring. When Philip's father comes on the scene he takes the time to put the pieces of track together. Once they are in place the little train can negotiate the twists and turns without hesitation. The rails make all the difference. It is from this viewpoint that we will be looking at the disciplines I am suggesting. We will see how they enable us to negotiate the difficulties and problems of life in a manner which will increase our growth and wholeness.

In case we think we have the power to heal ourselves by our own self-effort, let us be clear that these disciplines will not of themselves heal us. They will only put us in a place where God's life can flow into us and heal us. Without trying to compare these disciplines with those Richard Foster outlines in his classic, *Celebration of Discipline*, the principle he elucidates applies equally well to the disciplines we will be mentioning: 'God has given us the Disciplines of the spiritual life as a means of receiving His grace. The Disciplines allow us to place ourselves before God so that He can transform us . . . That is the way with the Spiritual Disciplines – they are a way of sowing to the Spirit . . . The Spiritual Disciplines can do nothing by themselves; they can only get us to the place where something can be done. They are God's means of grace.'[2]

The benefits of discipline

In our homes, our work-place, or in our everyday relationships some discipline is needed. Without it, life becomes chaotic and unproductive. Many times I have counselled people whose lives have lacked control in one or more areas. Sometimes it has been a woman who has not been able to schedule her work in the home. Her whole family suffers as a consequence. She is constantly hassled, over-worked, tired and joyless. Such people usually view discipline as an unnecessary burden. But their lives have become tedious and dull without it.

I once prayed with a man who procrastinated over every piece of work that did not have to be done immediately. Consequently he had letters piled high in his study. Nothing had been filed in months. The odd jobs around the house were left from year to year. He told me that he did not like doing any of these things and so left them. However, he was too depressed to enjoy the things he did like doing. I felt that anyone would be depressed and joyless with life in such chaos!

Applying a little discipline to life can change the way a person views himself in a surprising way. As a child my self-image was not very positive. Growing up with very little supervision or guidance from relatives, I never seemed able to achieve the things I dreamed of. I would start a project, come up against an obstacle and leave the enterprise unfinished. I constantly felt cheated and I envied those I read about in books who seemed able to accomplish so much. Sometimes it felt as if I was only partially living. When I got married I struggled along in rather a muddle. On one occasion when David had to be away from home for a month I had the opportunity of staying in the home of a woman who had had five children and lived in a large house. The whole neighbourhood knew the way to her front door and there always seemed to be someone sitting in her kitchen being cheered up with a cup of tea. Her home was always clean. The washing hung on the line twice a week. The cooking got done on Fridays and we ate a huge roast every Sunday. Her life seemed to be full and purposeful. After living in her home for a month I tried to model myself on this amazing person. Gradually I began to realise more of the things I dreamed of. Slowly over the years I have found that the more I have practised the disciplines we will be outlining the more my self-image has improved and my sense of achievement has grown.

These disciplines also have many other good spin-offs. Our church has an early-morning prayer meeting every day and it is a strong temptation to turn over and go back to sleep when the alarm goes at 6.30 a.m. But on those days that I delay that particular gratification and go first to the prayer time I find I also have time to get to the local pool to swim before breakfast. These days are by far my most productive days. I feel right with God. My energy level is higher. My mind is more alert. I accomplish more and I sleep better the next night. The benefits are good!

The disciplines in relationships

Our growth and maturity are closely linked to our dialogue with other people. Therefore the use of the disciplines in our relationships will be a major factor in our growth. Some of the richest moments of our lives will be experienced as we relate with others. Conversely some of the greatest pain will be endured in the process of relating. These experiences can add to our lives or demean them according to the disciplines we do or do not employ.

However much we try, close relationships will always incur some misunderstandings. We experience growth when we work through these together; learning to forgive and be forgiven. However, growth is by-passed when people are afraid to confront the problems as they occur and settle instead for peace, even a pseudo-peace. John Powell suggests that many people settle for a truce rather than a real relationship.[3] I once said, from the platform, that I thought keeping the peace at all costs was detrimental to a good relationship. Several people challenged me later and expressed the opinion that it was a very important and a Christian thing to keep the peace in a marriage. Many people mistakenly think that studiously avoiding conflict is the right way to live. But then they wonder why, over the years, they seem to have drifted away from each other.

A couple of years ago a middle-aged man contacted me. He was weeping. He told me that his marriage was coming apart and he did not know what he could do to save it. Later, seeing him together with his wife, I realised that two really nice people had, over the years, drifted apart. They had become strangers living under the same roof. Both had found it very difficult to share their real feelings with one another. They had not realised how important the disciplines of communication and dedication to truth must be in a good marriage. By keeping more of their thoughts and feelings to themselves they gradually knew less and less of each other until now they were experiencing real pain in their loneliness. They had both put off facing the difficult issue of their increasing isolation in the pursuit of peace at all costs. And it had nearly cost them their marriage.

However, once they decided to confront the problem the healing began, although it was many months before this was recognised by either of them. After two years of hard work, they at last began to reap the rewards of putting the disciplines we shall be mentioning into action.

Loving someone also means that it is right to speak the truth plainly from time to time, even though that truth may hurt the other person. It is painful for me when my husband, David, reads one of my manuscripts and then gives it back to me, saying that my argument is weak or confused and it needs re-writing. Truth may be difficult to receive but it will only be harmful when the aim is to diminish the other person. 'Wounds from a friend can be trusted' (Pr.27:6). It is, nevertheless, not always easy to speak the truth to a friend when you know it will wound them. Yet sometimes to withhold the truth is also to withhold an opportunity for growth.

Recently I spent a week at a conference with two of my daughters and their children. I usually sat with my family at the meetings and had one or other of my grandsons on my lap. Many people we knew were attending the same conference and one person spent the week feeling very upset. She had various explanations for her tearfulness but I felt that all these explanations were an avoidance of the truth. I knew that she was not purposely avoiding this but simply protecting herself from the pain of it. For several days I wondered which was the kindest thing to do; to keep silent and go along with the superficial explanations she was giving me, or speak out what I thought to be the truth and so risk hurting her. Paul talks about 'speaking the truth in love' (Eph.4:15). Some speak truth without love and this is cruel. Others feel that love prevents them from speaking the truth. I decided that if I really loved this girl and valued her growth I should tell her the truth. The circumstances of her life were not ideal and I knew that seeing the close and easy relationship I enjoyed with my daughters was probably stirring up sadness and longing within her. I told her this and explained that although her particular situation was a very sad one, neither I nor anyone else could change it. However, it was perfectly natural and understandable to grieve over the loss of one of the most important relationships of one's life. Grieving over loss is part of the healing process when it is done honestly and openly, but to evade the truth, as she was doing, would not be healing for her. It was very hard for my young friend to receive this but I think that in her heart she knew I wanted the best for her. Some weeks later she thanked me for speaking to her as I had. Although it had been extremely painful at the time, it proved to be a point of growth for her.

My colleague, Prue Bedwell and I have, over the past three years, spent many hours travelling, speaking and counselling together. We often laughingly tell people that our backgrounds and temperaments are so different that it is as if we come from different planets. This has meant that our relationship has not been naturally easy. It has been something we have had to work at. We have tried to employ the discipline of truthfulness with one another and when we have used it the relationship has grown in understanding and matured. When we have not, the hidden agenda has created a wall between us. Relating has become hard and unrewarding work. It means that, however uncomfortable it is, feelings have to be brought out in the open and talked about. Bad feelings must not be allowed to smoulder on unexpressed.

I was speaking at a conference recently when a lady came up to me. With tears in her eyes she said, 'I want one of those,' and pointed at Prue. 'I would like to have a friend like that,' she explained. She could most probably have that kind of relationship if she was prepared to commit herself to the disciplines involved. These things rarely fall into our laps ready-made. The same goes for a good marriage partnership. Daily discipline is involved and only those who are prepared to live this way will reap the benefits of a growing and maturing relationship.

The disciplines in the life of Jesus

Since Jesus is the perfect model for our lives it is good to look briefly at how He utilised all the disciplines we will be looking at. Jesus consistently *deferred gratifying His own personal needs* in order to achieve His Father's will. At the beginning of His ministry we find Him in the desert where He had been led by the Spirit to be tempted. Although He had been fasting for forty days and nights He was still able to delay appeasing His pangs of hunger. He refused to use His supernatural power to gratify His bodily appetites (Matt.4:2).

He also suffered the hardship of having no proper home to live in. He challenged one would-be disciple on his willingness to endure physical hardship by saying: 'Foxes have holes and birds of the air have nests, but the Son of Man has nowhere to lay his head' (Matt.8:20).

Jesus must often have felt extremely tired – as we are expressly told in John 4 verse 6 – and yet we frequently find Him giving up the gratification of rest to pray early in the morning (Luke 5:16, Mark 1:35). Effective prayer always requires discipline.

We never find Jesus shifting responsibility for His life onto others. The phrase, 'You made me do it,' is never heard from His lips. Instead *He took responsibility for His own actions*, which is another important discipline. Although He often acted out of compassion for the crowds, He was not manipulated by others or by their needs. He was led by His Father and said and did what His Father told Him to say and do (John 8:28). He did this even when He would be misunderstood by His dearest friends. When Lazarus was taken desperately ill He stayed two days in the same place and did not rush to heal him, in spite of the urgings of Mary and Martha (John 11:6).

Long-term devotion to His divine commission proved His *dedication to the Father's will* for His life. This is the essence of *commitment to growth and maturity*. He spent many hours instructing and encouraging His disciples so that they would grow and mature. In His interaction with these men He frequently spent time *communicating* with them. They were not left in ignorance of His plans and purposes. He was not afraid of *speaking the truth* even when it was difficult for them to receive it or it would cause them pain.

This life of discipline and obedience was tested to its limits in the garden of Gethsemane. We find Jesus agonising in prayer as He contemplated the horrific task which lay before Him. Not only would the physical suffering be terrible but the emotional and spiritual suffering would be appalling. It seems to have been almost more than He could bear, to contemplate the weight of sin He was about to carry and the separation He knew this would cause between Himself and His beloved Father. The decision to lay His life down was His. Had He not said that no one could take His life from Him; He would lay it down of His own accord? 'I have authority to lay it down and authority to take it up again' (John 10:18). It was a costly decision but finally He cried out to God, 'Yet not my will, but yours be done' (Luke 22:42). He chose *to lay down His own life* and take the path of suffering *in order to achieve the greatest victory* of all time. C.S. Lewis writes, 'There are two kinds of people in the end: those who say to God, "Thy will be done", and those to whom God says, in the end, "Thy will be done".'[4]

Not only did Jesus spend many hours alone in prayer but He was in constant touch with His Father and was able to say: 'I and the Father are one' (John 10:30). He unceasingly *celebrated His Father's presence*. As the Son of God there was no obstacle to Jesus practising each of these disciplines. They will not be so easy for us. Nevertheless, their use could mean the difference between immaturity and maturity.

Techniques for growth

Life is a series of problems for us all. The way in which we confront these problems could be occasions of growth, or they could cause us to remain emotional and spiritual adolescents for the rest of our lives. James spelt this out quite clearly: 'Consider it pure joy, my brothers, whenever you face trials of many kinds, because you know that the testing of your faith develops perseverance. Perseverance must finish its work so that you may be mature and complete, not lacking anything' (James 1:2–4).

The disciplines necessary for growth are quite simple, yet very few people actually put them into practice. Those who truly desire to grow should lose no time in implementing them. We may not be immediately successful. Failure may occur, but this can either be a discouragement or an encouragement to try again. John Powell points out that 'Once a commitment has been made, the main obstacle to perseverance is failure'.[5] The pathway to success is often paved with failures. Ninety per cent of success is said to be built on failure. No one learns to ride a bicycle or to roller skate without falling a few times. The desire to learn or the commitment to the task will keep us trying.

For someone whose healing and development is blocked by a habitual defence mechanism, or 'survival kit', each one of these disciplines will be a key to removing the blockage and placing us in a position where healing may occur. Should we become slack and neglect to use the disciplines the process will grind to a stand-still. It is a good idea, therefore, to review our lives every now and again to ensure nothing is being overlooked.

Exercises

1. When you read or hear the word 'discipline' what is your immediate reaction? Share it with the group.

2. If you had a negative reaction, spend a few minutes now in silent prayer and meditation allowing God to show you the reason for the bad feeling.

3. Ask God to show you any area of your life in which you

need to implement more discipline. Or, conversely, any area in which you are imposing too rigid a structure.

4. Share with your group/friend/journal anything God may have shown you.

5. Perhaps there is something in your past history which is still influencing your response to discipline and you would like this dealt with. Spend some time now ministering to one another.

If you have become aware of some irrational beliefs about discipline because of past experience or teaching, these need to be renounced. Help from another Christian may be necessary to break the power of these beliefs in the Name of Jesus.

6. Last, look for one or more passages of Scripture which contain positive teaching about discipline. Read this aloud and then pray that God's truth will take root and wrong thinking will be corrected.

3. DEFERRING GRATIFICATION

'There was a man who had two sons. The younger one said to his father, "Father, give me my share of the estate". So he divided his property between them' (Luke 15:11,12).

This young man was bored. He was buried alive in the country working on his father's estate. His older brother was moody and serious and not very good company. He longed for the excitement of the big city. Finally, rather than suffer such boredom a moment longer, he went to his father and demanded his share of the estate immediately. The father, well aware of his son's growing discontent, gave in to his demands, hoping the boy would have a taste of the world and quickly realise its emptiness. The son collected all his money, waved goodbye and set out for the bright lights of a distant city.

Inexperienced and naïve, he went on a spending spree. He tasted all the fantastic things he had previously only heard about. Wine, women and song filled his days and nights while his pockets grew empty. The day came when he pulled out his wallet for the last time only to find his wealth had been squandered away. He was then forced to take stock but there was no stock to take. Whilst he had been engrossed in living it up there had been a major famine. Everyone had been affected by it and there was nothing left over for a down-and-out foreigner. The young man experienced real hunger and cold for the first time in his life. Desperate for food and shelter, he hired himself out to a local man. But how the situation had changed. No longer the boss's precious young son who casually oversaw others at work, he was now reduced to a state worse than that of the pigs he was sent to feed. At least they had their food to eat. He had nothing. Starvation and death stared him in the face.

What went wrong? How could such a thing have occurred? It was all very easy. The younger son wanted his pleasure immediately. He could not defer gratifying his desires until the time when he would inherit his wealth. For many of us this discipline is the hardest of all to put into practice. It does not come naturally unless it has been instilled into us early in life by wise parents. Even then, youthful rebellion will sometimes cause children to choose the exact opposite to the way they have been trained by parents.

The meaning of deferring gratification

It is not an easy discipline to grasp, so before we can appreciate how it helps us to mature we must first try and understand what it means.

The *Dictionary of the Social Sciences* defines 'deferred gratification' as a 'self-imposed postponement of gratification'.[1] It is the decision to plan one's life in such a way that one faces and deals with the pain and problems first, in order to experience pleasure more fully later. As one of my daughters put it when trying to sort out a difficult situation, 'Pain now, pleasure later'.

The process of planning one's life in this way will involve a person in the two difficult activities of postponement and confrontation.

Postponement

When we defer gratification it means that occasionally something we want to do or say will have to be postponed in order to achieve some higher or better purpose.

The prodigal son in our story could not wait until his father had died or retired to inherit his share of the estate. Had he waited, his share would have provided somewhere to live, a ready-made job to support a wife and family and, most precious of all, his father's special blessing. But like many of us he could not take such an objective long-term view of life. He could only think impulsively and selfishly of what he wanted right now.

When I was at our boarding-school our meals were not always very appetising. However, the school cook excelled herself on Sundays. She would have made Egon Ronay proud. The only problem was that I disliked vegetables. I used to keep the best of the meat and the crispiest of the potatoes to be eaten at the end. Once the vegetables were eaten, and with pleasure heightened by the anticipation, I would enjoy the last mouthful with relish. Deferred gratification!

Confrontation

Postponing the good until later will mean, conversely, having to confront the not so good or the most difficult earlier. The less enjoyable tasks, the painful problems and the tiresome monotonies of life have a tendency to be put off or ignored by us all. To defer gratification means that these unpleasant things will be addressed in some disciplined way and a resolution sought.

Every year our church runs a 'Communion in Marriage' course. Homework is given to the couples who come to encourage their communication with each other. It is not easy to sit down and discuss issues that have been left un-aired for many years. But many couples appreciate being forced to confront some difficult areas together that might have otherwise remained untouched. Many testify to a deeper relationship as a result. Some, however, have found it too painful and have felt unable to attend the second part of the course.

Reasons for the difficulties

This discipline appears to be a particularly difficult one for some people.

Our culture

The materialistic culture in which we live does not encourage this way of life. It is too easy to buy whatever we want by instalments. 'Buy now — pay later,' is the motto. The Easy Access card is aptly named. We can have our material wants met almost instantly. This does not encourage postponement of pleasure until the less agreeable task of earning the money is fulfilled. Society today does not help us delay gratification. I once saw an advertisement for a new model car. It read, 'Pursue pleasure faster!' Perhaps the first thing we need to do is to delay a moment in the midst of our activity and take time to confront our unreal way of life. Are we missing the best and the full blessing by our crazy pursuit of wealth and pleasure?

A few years ago I met a very successful estate agent. He worked for a big firm in London and spent a good deal of life travelling around the country inspecting big properties that were coming on the market. For many years he had had a longing to change the direction of his life, go back to college and learn how to be a carpenter. It sounded like a fanciful dream to his friends until he actually made the brave decision to take early retirement and make his dream come true. He had to confront some difficulties first but eventually was able to achieve the desire of his heart. Now at fifty-six he is back at college learning carpentry. Because his whole way of life has radically changed he and his wife have had to work through some difficult problems. By opting out of the materialistic rat-race, however, he will in the end achieve a great deal of satisfaction and gratification.

Poor parenting

Our culture has not helped us to implement this discipline. Sometimes our parents have not helped us either. Parents who have not developed the capacity to defer gratification themselves will not be able to pass it on to their children. Children learn through visual, audio, and practical means. They need to watch something being done, have it explained to them and then have a go themselves. It is the best way to learn and should begin early in life. It needs to be a natural part of the family life-style and experienced as a good way of living. If a particular life-style is beneficial and pays good dividends then a child will most likely continue to live that way when he is adult and responsible for his own life.

We were by no means perfect parents to our four daughters. There were times when we failed to teach them to delay gratification. However, living as we did in the beautiful country of Chile, we always tried to take Saturdays off and spend them by a lake or beach. This meant we all had to get our tasks for the weekend done by Friday evening. I had to get the shopping, washing and cooking done: David had to finish his preparations for Sunday; the children had to complete their homework and anything else that needed to be ready for the following week. After all this hard work we were ready to enjoy our day off. We felt we had earned the break and none of the pleasure was spoiled by the pressure of unfinished business.

Our oldest daughter used the same method to get through her school and university exams. She had to work extra hard, having been educated in a Spanish system and only returning to England at fourteen. She had also missed out on English television and quickly became a fan. She found that by scheduling her viewing she could make the television an incentive for her work. She would set herself a certain amount of work and get down to it with energy having promised herself the reward of an hour of television later.

The ability to defer gratification seems to come easily to some people, but the reason they develop the capacity and others do not is not fully understood. However, the quality of parenting received is thought by many to be an important influence. An undisciplined parent cannot preach successfully what he does not practise. How can he punish a child for not doing his homework when he never completes the odd jobs around the house? How can he live a chaotic life and then smack a child for losing or forgetting things? A thoughtless parent will not take time to be with the child long enough to encourage the practice of the discipline. Children are too immature to do it alone. Time is the most precious commodity any of us has, yet many parents exchange so many lesser things for time.

Only as parents postpone the gratification of doing their own thing and spend time with a child will that child learn the important disciplines of life. He will simultaneously receive a sense of his own value. 'This feeling of being valuable is a cornerstone of self-discipline because when one considers oneself valuable one will take care of oneself in all ways that are necessary.'[2] Time is needed to think constructively and objectively on how to be a good parent. It is easier to seek a quick solution or do the obvious thing than to sit down and plan a way of parenting that will benefit the child in the long term.

Inner pain

Another reason for a person having difficulty implementing this discipline may be inner discomfort that demands alleviation. Pain of any sort cries out for attention. A person will instinctively focus attention on internal or external discomfort and seek ways of relieving it immediately. Short-term measures may then be taken which may well be detrimental to the person concerned.

Janice was such a person. After a year of anxiety with a very sick child and an unfaithful husband, her doctor prescribed valium. It succeeded in calming her panic attacks but because the problems did not go away she was soon forced into increasing the dosage to give the same relief. Although the valium masked the anxiety it did not solve the problems she was living with. These difficulties continued and her need of the valium increased until she realised that addiction was now added to her list of problems. A short-term solution had created a long-term problem.

During her stay in a mental institution the successful American TV producer, Barbara Gordon, worked with a therapist every day. Again and again she begged this woman to give her some pills to help alleviate the emotional pain she was enduring. But Julie, her counsellor, refused. Barbara begged for relief. She offered money, her beach house, anything she had, if Julie would only end her suffering. But Julie always refused, telling her again and again that to have a lasting recovery she had to take nothing. Pills couldn't bring back her life. Only she could do that. It was her best chance. Instead of giving her a pill, Julie would make Barbara go back to her childhood and scrutinise her personal way of life. All her life Barbara had shoved so many disagreeable things aside, ignored things she did not want to see. Her own innate repressive mechanism, combined with the insidious repressive functioning of valium had made her worse than Scarlett O'Hara.[3]

Mandy is another person who will seek a quick solution to her inner pain and in so doing continually jeopardises her future. She has a fear of being left alone or of being abandoned by her friends. Whenever these lonely feelings surface she cannot suffer them for any length of time but looks for a way of allaying them. Whatever she is doing, she will drop it and run to the phone or to the home of a friend. For as long as she can remember these fears have controlled her and rarely has she been able to put off the gratification of having them relieved immediately. She will put off work and study, important things for her future happiness, in order to feel better for a short while.

Inner pain can, therefore, make this discipline difficult to put into practice. Nevertheless, whilst it is ignored growth and maturity will never be achieved.

Fear

Equally, fear can be a major factor in a person's life. Fear of another's anger, fear of confrontation, fear of loss, or rejection can be the cause of someone never facing up to a problem. The fear is bigger and stronger than the desire to resolve the difficulty. Peace or acceptance may seem more important than the discomfort of confrontation.

I have inherited my father's love of a peaceful life. I can also remember my mother's angry outbursts and the discomfort I felt. This combination has inclined me to shy away from confrontations with David or the children. Consequently the normal problems and frustrations of family life were often not discussed in an open, frank way. David may have raised some issue but I would ignore it. I would swallow my feelings, change the subject and think I was smoothing things over. For many years it seemed the best way to behave, until I was challenged by a friend and forced to examine my behaviour. By not confronting and dealing with family problems, I was blocking, not only my own growth, but the growth of intimacy within the family.

The importance of deferring gratification

As we have already said, life is full of problems. The way in which we confront these or fail to do so could mean the difference between growth and shrinkage, insight and blindness, happiness and misery, order and chaos, mental health and mental illness.

It creates the right environment for healing

Many psychologists feel that this tendency to avoid problems and emotional pain forms the basis for all mental illness. Some people will go to quite extraordinary lengths to avoid problems and the suffering they cause. They may even try to exclude reality by building elaborate fantasies in which to live.

Christopher Kinkaid was such a person. He had suffered the most appalling abuse as a child and as a result he had fragmented and split into seven different personalities. Dr Michaels, his psychiatrist, uncovered the horrific truth of Christopher's past. 'When Christopher was a little boy, he didn't want it to happen to him, so he made up Richard and let Richard be the victim. "It's not happening to me. It's happening to someone else," he said to himself. And every time something bad would happen, it happened to someone else - to Timmy or Sissy or James or Jackie − not to him. Christopher had defended himself against human brutality. He had fragmented, split apart to survive.'[4] The book tells the story of Christopher's bravery and Dr Michaels' tenacity as together they confronted abuse, brutality, neglect, long-term incest and sexual molestation in Christopher's childhood. Gradually and painfully he came out of denial and into mental health. Both Christopher and his doctor had to work hard for many years. During that time they deferred gratification in many different ways. The painful truth had to be confronted and there was no rest

for either of them until it was done. Few of us will have
suffered to the same degree as Christopher. Nevertheless,
whatever the problem, healing for all of us will be dependent
upon this discipline being implemented.

When this discipline becomes a way of life the environment for confronting pain is created. A person becomes
accustomed to dealing with difficult issues immediately and
delaying pleasure or peace until these are resolved. Gradually
the courage is found to look behind the 'survival kit' at the
inner pain. Healing then becomes a possibility.

It aids growth

My friend, Janice, who became addicted to valium, was
eventually taken into hospital. Now, four years later, she
knows that problems do not simply go away with a pill or
a drink. Her difficulties are long-term ones and by facing
them and owning them she has been able to find a way of
living with them and coping with the pain. The process has
matured her considerably.

In the ministry of prayer counselling this discipline is vital
for both counsellor and counsellee. If growth is the objective
of counselling, then the delay of gratification must be
implemented. At first a counsellee may need help to use the
discipline but the more it is practised the greater the growth.

It deepens relationships

Intimacy in relationships is only achieved through self-
disclosure, sharing of feelings as well as opinions and the
giving and receiving of forgiveness. None of these things
is easy. The ability to postpone longed-for peace and to
confront pain is called for. We all desire peace and happiness
but if they are gained through shortcuts and cheating they
will be only imitations of the real thing. The joy of real
relationships is only achieved with time and hard work.

It ultimately brings peace, happiness and fulfilment

Peace of heart is achieved when the painful wounds of the soul have first been uncovered and healed. Fulfilment is experienced at the completion of some hard work. Ultimately happiness will be found when we have completed our lives here, having lived them to the full, without resorting to lies, subterfuges, shortcuts and avoidances.

Last year *The Sower* magazine printed an interview with Garvan Byrne, a twelve-year-old boy with the body of a five year old who had a bone marrow disease. In this interview he talked courageously about his illness and the possibility of dying. He said, 'One time I was talking to Mummy about it, and she told me about my illness and what could happen, and I wasn't afraid. I said to her: "I'm glad I'm talking about it with you, because I feel better." Some children might not feel very happy talking about dying and things – it might make them afraid. But in my point of view, I find it helps me to talk about it. It helps me to bring out my courage and things'.[5]

When Garvan died, soon after this interview, his mother must have been so glad that she had not avoided that painful subject. Facing up to death in this way helped him to live his short life to the full. Many people live much longer than Garvan but could miss the depth of living he experienced because of their concern to avoid suffering.

It is a way of loving oneself and one's neighbour

If Mandy (mentioned earlier) can put off running here, there, and everywhere to alleviate her bad feelings of loneliness and begin to face her problems; if she can work at changing the self-destructive patterns in her life she will find her self-respect and self-acceptance growing. Once she begins to apply herself to study and work her future will become more secure and in that way she will have done great good to herself.

I have a friend who has been unpunctual all her life. She has always wanted to do just one more thing in her house or her garden before leaving for an appointment. The pleasure of taking out one more weed has been hard to delay! Consequently she has usually arrived five or ten minutes late. She has many friends and values her relationships but recently she received a shock when she felt God telling her that she was a hypocrite to say she valued others and then be late for an appointment with them. She felt so convicted that she set about changing the bad habit immediately. It meant that she had to live with the discomfort of leaving some job undone and postpone the pleasure of finishing it until later. Her efforts at being more punctual were amply rewarded by the obvious delight and enthusiasm of her friends.

Encouraging the development of this discipline

If it is important that we learn how to defer gratification, we must find ways of encouraging this discipline in our lives. Various factors will aid its development.

Support

If a person finds the postponement of pleasure, peace or relief and the confrontation of pain, problems and difficulties very hard, then he will need help and support to develop this discipline. This help may come from a friend, a group or perhaps it will come in a counselling relationship.

Ruth is a young woman who can defer gratification in some areas of her life quite easily, but she has a problem when it comes to saying 'no'. Frequently she will say 'yes' when she would like to say 'no', or even when she knows she should say 'no'. She cannot face the bad feelings that saying 'no' arouses in her. So she takes the easy route and then pays for it afterwards by being pushed for time and exhausted. She has begun to deal with the underlying problems and receive prayer for healing. However, she needs firm support from friends in her efforts to change. For example, if she knows she is going to be in a situation where she will be tempted to say 'yes' when she should say 'no', she will tell a friend about it. The act of telling someone seems to strengthen her resolve to do the right thing. She still has to make the difficult choice but the support makes it easier.

' All growth needs support to begin with. Even a young sapling needs a supporting stake in the early days of taking root.

Time

The healing encounter with God may be sudden and dramatic and this may cause us to expect an equally quick transformation. But growth, as always, takes time. If the ability to defer gratification has been absent from a person's life, it will take a while to learn it.

Motivation

In order to implement this discipline, a person first has to be convinced it is a better way to live. My friend Ruth was not at all sure to begin with. She had convinced herself that to say 'yes' to everyone's requests for help was being more loving – even more Christ-like. Eventually she realised that to say 'yes' in order to gratify her need to please everyone was selfish. It could involve her in saying 'yes' to someone when the right response was 'no'. She saw the bondage she was under and wanted to be free. Her motivation was to be transformed and changed so that she would really be more like Jesus, who was free to say 'no', and often did.

As with all the disciplines, there has to be a good strong incentive to defer gratification. I can face pain if by doing so I, or others I love, will benefit in some way. I will go to the dentist because I know the discomfort I experience will help me keep my teeth for longer. Deferring gratification has many benefits for ourselves and those we love. It really is the best way to live.

By ignoring this discipline the prodigal son involved himself and his family in much suffering. However, he did eventually come to his senses and he started on the road to recovery when he put into practice our next discipline.

Exercises

1. Explain 'deferring gratification' in your own words.

2. Find an example of this discipline in the life of Jesus.

3. Share an instance in your own life when you have implemented this discipline and one when you have failed to do so. Compare the outcome of these two experiences.

4. No one finds this an easy discipline but for some it is very hard. Spend some time in silent prayer asking God to show you any reason why this may be particularly difficult for you. Share your findings with your group/friend/journal.

5. Is there an issue in your life at present which you are not confronting? If so, what prevents you dealing with the problem or difficulty? Is there any way in which your group/friend can help you overcome the blockage?

6. Pray for one another. If the block is fear or insecurity caused by past bad experience suggest the person recounts this experience aloud to Jesus. Give plenty of time for the feelings surrounding the memory to be explored, and

expressed, if possible. Some forgiveness may need to be released. Ask Jesus to bring some healing to the memory and give Him time to do this. It is possible that the past bad experience may have caused the person to make some type of inner vow, or form an irrational belief that may now need to be renounced.

4.   TAKING RESPONSIBILITY

'When he came to his senses, he said, ''How many of my father's hired men have food to spare, and here I am starving to death! I will set out and go back to my father and say to him: Father, I have sinned against heaven and against you. I am no longer worthy to be called your son; make me like one of your hired men''' (Luke 15:17–19).

One evening, after another lonely and miserable day, the prodigal son, cold and clutching his empty stomach, huddled in a corner and thought about his predicament. 'What am I doing here?' he asked himself. 'My brother is living in comfort and even my father's servants are eating square meals. I will go back home and tell my father how stupid I have been – I have been guilty of sin against God and my father.'

The young man was totally alone in the world with no one to take responsibility for him. There was no point in wasting energy blaming others. That would not get him out of his awful plight. He could have blamed his older brother for being such a bore or his father for letting him have his inheritance on demand. But he knew it would have done no good. His frequent use of the little word 'I' shows he had decided to take responsibility for his circumstances. First by owning the problem, then by thinking of a solution and then by putting the solution into effect.

Taking proper responsibility

This discipline is fundamental to growth. Without it we will remain immature for life. If a child has been gradually introduced to taking responsibility for himself he will later be able to exercise the discipline quite naturally. However, if this has not been a natural part of his upbringing it can be a difficult discipline to utilise later in life.

Furthermore, it is difficult for some people to differentiate between what is their proper responsibility and what is not. Some react neurotically to conflict and problems by automatically assuming too much responsibility, others respond, equally neurotically, by blaming everyone else for their difficulties. People usually lean towards one direction or the other, although they may not have a full-blown neurosis. In a room full of comparatively healthy people it would be possible to ask a few questions and place them on one or other side of the responsibility line: some taking too much responsibility for the events of their lives and others too little.

Betty suffers from a very low self-image. Her worth depends largely on achievement. She works hard at that. When something goes wrong her immediate response will be, 'It's my fault'. Talking about her childhood she will continually explain how difficult she was, and still is, to live with. Betty takes an inappropriate amount of responsibility for the bad experiences in her life.

At the other extreme, Maggie sees herself as being on the receiving end of people's unkindness and thoughtlessness. She once told me that her teenage daughter had been very cruel to her by leaving home suddenly. 'She was so cruel and thoughtless. She just left the house without a word to *me*.' I learned from another source that in fact Maggie had had a violent row with her daughter and had thrown her out of the house. She was right in saying her daughter had suddenly left home without a word to her, and she may also have been thoughtless, as many teenagers are. But Maggie side-stepped taking any responsibility for her daughter's leaving when in fact she really did have some responsibility for it.

Both these positions demonstrate immaturity. It is a problem which must be addressed if growth is to occur. People like Betty who tend to see themselves as blameworthy for all their difficulties are at least moving in the direction of taking responsibility, even if they overdo it. In a counselling situation the Bettys are easier to help, whereas the Maggies of this world will often try to evade owning their problems. John Powell suggests that most people are like Maggie. They grew up as 'blamers', accusing others of making them angry. It is hard for most of us to acknowledge that our actions and reactions are not caused by others but rather by something in us. Yet this is always the case. He writes, 'If I can only cross over the line that separates the "blamers" from those who accept the full responsibility for their behaviour, it will probably be the most mature thing I have ever done. At least it will bring me into an honest contact with reality, and this is the only way to grow into a mature human being.'[1]

Today Christian churches the world over are becoming more aware of spiritual forces, both demonic and divine. There is rightly an increase in the deliverance ministry as we see the rise of Satan worship. However, it is sometimes hard for the Christian to find the correct balance between having something cast out of him by others and his taking responsibility for rectifying his behaviour throught discipline. Partly due to the fast food, instant culture we live in, many Christians are looking for quick solutions to their problems. The deliverance ministry is Biblical and of great benefit to those who really need it, but there is a tendency for some to hunt for curses from generations past and ancestral demons to blame for normal difficulties common to everyone. These come from the old nature. Such works of the flesh need putting to death (Col.3:5–11). The discipline of taking responsibility for self is integral to the process of sanctification: of dying to self and living to God. Paul said, 'I die every day' (1 Cor.15:31). There are no 'quickie' solutions. It's the disciplined work of a life-time.

Of course the same could be said for the ministry of inner healing. Some view the prayer for healing of past hurts as the only needed ministry. They hope that God will miraculously change the attitudes and patterns of a life-time without involving the person concerned in any effort. As we have already implied, prayer for inner healing can be very effective when it is part of an ongoing process of growth. It only becomes counter-productive if it encourages a person to avoid taking responsibility for growing up and changing.

There is no doubt that the more we implement this discipline the greater will be our growth in maturity. It is helpful, therefore, to understand what taking proper responsibility involves and how we can use it more effectively.

Owning-up

It entails owning our thoughts, feelings, decisions, words, actions and problems. It means taking responsibility for them and the appropriate blame or credit. John Powell encourages us to make 'I statements' because when we do this we are taking responsibility for our own reactions. We may not understand fully all that has shaped our reactions. We do know, however, that our reactions have been the result of something within us. Therefore, when we make an 'I statement', we are admitting this to ourselves and to others.[2]

It is not always easy to take responsibility for our opinions and our decisions. People find the possibility of being wrong very threatening. Within a marriage relationship there will always be areas of conflict that need to be sorted out. A common one is who navigates the car and who takes the blame after a wrong turn! We eventually solved this difficulty by my husband, David, having responsibility for the driving and getting us to the place without mishap, whilst I have the responsibility for mapping out the route and guiding us there without getting lost. At first I found it very difficult to accept the blame when I took a wrong turning, until one day I was quite obviously mistaken and could find no way of wriggling out of the responsibility. As I hesitated, I felt something within me relax and I found myself saying, 'I'm sorry, that was my fault. It should have been a left turn, not a right one.' One of our girls gasped in the back seat and David turned to me with a look of amazement. 'That's OK, darling,' he said. It was so easy! Taking such responsibility has made previously difficult journeys pleasant and peaceful occasions.

Living in the present

Taking responsibility also means living in the present. The problem presently causing difficulty may have originated in the past. A mother, father, spouse, teacher or an employer may have been the actual cause of the problem. However, at this moment in time the problem belongs to the person who is troubled by it. Only he or she has the power and the energy to solve it. To harp back to the past and apportion blame, however true that may be, will not help resolve the difficulty. When attention is focused on the past the energy for finding a solution in the present is frequently missing. An answer will only be found by moving the energy and focus to the immediate predicament.

Bad feelings towards those perceived to have caused the problem may have to be dealt with. But continually living in blame can never expel bad feelings. Feelings will only be changed by expressing them appropriately, forgiving the hurt and receiving God's healing.

Finding a solution

To take responsibility also involves finding a solution. Once a problem or difficulty has been owned by someone it then clearly becomes that person's responsibility to do something about it.

The following example may seem a trivial incident to someone who is battling against great odds to keep a marriage alive, or to someone who has lost a close relationship through a hurtful betrayal. Yet it seems that many a relationship, be it a marriage or a friendship, has foundered on such minor irritations and annoying habits. Unspoken resentments, lack of forgiveness and blame-shifting gradually produce an immovable barrier. A solution to the mountain of problems is never found because no problem is ever owned by anyone.

Tidiness is a common difficulty in most homes. Many wives complain that their husbands never put their clothes away. For twenty years I protested at my husband's apparent inability to put his dirty clothes in the linen basket which was kept in the bathroom. I tried leaving them on the floor, getting angry, pleading. But nothing seemed to work. David would simply repeat the same answer: 'The clothes' basket is too far away'. He seemed oblivious to the fact that this was becoming a major problem! One morning, as I bent down for probably the two thousandth time and picked up some article of his clothing, I muttered angrily, 'Why can't he change?' Suddenly the thought came into my head: 'Because he doesn't have a problem.' I had the problem — not David. It didn't worry him — only me. As I stood by the bed and absorbed this revelation I went one step further. 'If it is my problem not his, then what am I going to do about it?' Once I had established this fact the next step seemed easy and I couldn't think why it had taken me twenty years to arrive at it. I went into the bathroom, picked up the clothes' basket and moved it into the bedroom. Problem solved! The reason I had not discovered this practical solution years earlier was because I did not see it as my problem. The solution was within reach once I took responsibility for the impasse. But taking responsibility is a discipline that can be difficult to implement even in ordinary domestic situations.

Reasons for the difficulty

There are a number of reasons why this discipline is particularly difficult for some people to employ.

Inappropriate past teaching

Just the other day I watched a toddler hit her head on the corner of a table and the mother quite automatically smacked the table and said, 'Naughty table!' When she did this she was unknowingly teaching the child to put the responsibility for her actions and the consequences of her actions onto someone or something outside of herself. In other words she was learning, from an early age, the unhealthy practice of blame-shifting — 'Someone out there is to blame for my bad feelings.' A child will not naturally take responsibility for himself. It is something that will develop with maturity as he witnesses others do it and as he is taught to do it himself.

Adam and Eve, in the garden of Eden, both fell into the trap of blame-shifting. After they had eaten the forbidden fruit they hid from God. But He found them and called to them. He asked them if they had eaten from the tree that He had commanded them not to. First Adam blamed God for what had happened. 'The woman *you* put here with me . . .' Then he blamed the woman. '*She* gave me some fruit . . .' Although he does eventually include himself in the activity, it is not before he has made it clear to all parties that it wasn't really his fault — the responsibility lay elsewhere. Eve does the same. She shifts the blame onto the serpent. 'The *serpent* deceived me, and I ate.' In other words, 'It wasn't really my fault either because he made me do it.' (Gen.3:11–13). Without hesitation they had both shifted responsibility for their action onto others. One result of the fall is that we all find difficulty taking responsibility for ourselves in an appropriate way.

Killer statements

So often a child can be fed erroneous information by a thoughtless parent. Angry outbursts, sometimes referred to as 'killer statements' can adversely affect a child's view of himself. 'You are driving me crazy.' 'I'm killing myself for you.' 'You make me sick.' 'You are a wicked child and God will punish you,' are some common ones. The immature child believes the 'all-powerful' parent and takes responsibility for causing other people's unhappiness. When the child becomes an adult he/she may be plagued by groundless feelings of guilt.

Short-sighted parenting

A far-sighted parent will not deny his child the opportunity to take responsibility appropriate to his stage of development. He knows that by doing so he will give his son or daughter the chance to develop a healthy attitude towards himself and others.

The short-sighted parent, on the other hand, will rarely think of the consequences of over-protecting his offspring. He shields him from discomfort, covers for his mistakes and rescues him from every difficulty, even when he is old enough to cope with these situations and take the consequences. Thus the growing child has had no chance to feel his own weight and is being denied the possibility of developing this ability. When he eventually reaches adulthood and has to answer for his own mistakes he quickly starts looking for scapegoats. A father I know spent a great deal of time, energy and money rescuing his wayward son. Eventually a wise friend advised him to allow his son to suffer the consequences of his own actions. It was a hard task for this over-protective father but he did it and eventually had the joy of seeing his son 'come to his senses' and start acting in a more mature way.

Low self-esteem

Another reason for finding this discipline difficult is low self-esteem. A person with a poor self-image feels worthless. He will either weakly accept that he is always to blame and so feel even more worthless and depressed. Or he will protect the diminished, inferior inner-self by shifting the blame from himself and onto someone else. Already he feels totally worthless. He calculates that just one more bad mark against him will destroy him. This bad self-image usually goes back to the quality of mothering received. Mother's eyes are the beacon light of identity for a baby. Therefore a baby that perceived rejection, anger or depression in his mother's face will identify with these bad feelings. It is as if he has looked into a mirror and seen what he looks like – unacceptable, ugly, bad and worthless. These are the predominant feelings he holds about himself. They will cause him to construct a 'survival kit' which may on the one hand include guilt and the need to punish himself still further or, conversely, an avoidance of any guilt by projecting his bad feelings onto others so that he sees them as bad, and not himself.

Frank Lake gives us some understanding of the paranoid personality: 'His inmost being, through no fault of his own, is identified with emptiness, meaninglessness, inferiority, low self-esteem, emasculated powers, a weak and sickly human spirit . . . Until he can deflate his defensive pride by coming to terms with the hidden pain of his initial humiliation, nothing can reach him.' The paranoid patient 'cannot surrender this defence without encountering mental pain of great intensity. He would have to meet the naked terror of emptiness.'[3]

Obviously this acute form of paranoia needs professional attention. However, there are many hurting people who, because of their unhealed inner pain, do have trouble accepting blame which may rightly belong to them, although they may not suffer from a mental illness.

The importance of taking responsibility

For many reasons it is important that this discipline of taking responsibility should become an essential part of our lives.

No one can mature without it

If a person can learn to identify how much responsibility is his, pick that up and leave what is not, he will mature with rapidity. It is a vital discipline for growth. The most painful failures we have encountered during the years we have been counselling have been caused by the difficulty found in using this discipline. Either the counsellor is blamed for not understanding and not caring enough, or someone else, usually another family member, is blamed for causing the problem in the first place. The implication is always that if only other people would change the problems would disappear.

We worked for a while with a young girl who complained that her husband was to blame for her unhappiness. This seemed to indicate a marriage problem, so we began to see them together. At every session she complained that he did not do enough for her. He never brought her chocolates, for example. The next session she complained that he was thoughtless because now he was bringing her chocolates all the time! Whatever the poor man did to change was never good enough. She was sure he did it on purpose to hurt her. Every attempt to help her own her bad feelings and look at them was foiled. Eventually we realised that we had failed. She did not feel safe enough to dispense with the 'survival kit' and therefore the inner emptiness was not being healed. We kept going for months, hoping she would trust us enough to let us and God see her inner pain. She seemed unable to do this. Apparently her 'survival kit' was locked on like a suit of armour.

It encourages self-control

When another person is blamed for my feelings, thoughts or actions that person is granted a power over me he should not, and in fact, does not, really possess. That power of control is reclaimed by assuming responsibility for oneself. A human being has only as much control over another human being as he has been given. The Bible encourages Christians to produce the fruit of self-control in their lives (Gal.5:23). Taking appropriate responsibility for oneself will foster the development of that particular fruit.

Statements such as: 'She gave me a sleepless night', referring to a daughter living far from home; or 'My mother makes me feel guilty', from a son who has left home, are obviously impossible if one considers them. No one living some distance from another individual has power to affect his feelings. People create their own bad feelings by their thinking. John Powell quotes the sign that Eleanor Roosevelt kept posted on the wall of her office: 'No one can make you feel inferior, unless you give him permission.' He goes on to say, 'In fact, no one can make us feel or act in any certain way. Something in us always remains in charge of our emotional and behavioural reactions. Other persons, circumstances or situations may stimulate a reaction. We determine what that reaction will be.'[4]

One woman would sit in silence for most of her counselling session. When she was challenged on her lack of communication she accused her counsellor of making her silent. 'You make me frightened and then I can't speak,' she said. In fact her own reaction to her counsellor was making her silent and it would have been more truthful and responsible to have said, 'I feel frightened when I come here because I think you will reject me.' Continuing to blame the counsellor will keep her out of control and in a paralysed, non-healing place. Once she starts owning her feelings she will take back the control of her life and with that will come the possibility of growth. As John Powell writes, 'I will stunt my personal growth as long as I persist in this unwillingness to acknowledge my responsibility. Remember: *Growth begins where blaming ends.*'[5]

It lays a foundation for health

Having the responsibility for something usually means that we take more care of it. If one of my daughters visits me with her children I mostly leave her to care for them, but if she leaves them with me they become my responsibility. Then I focus my full attention on their welfare.

It is the same with ourselves. Once we assume the responsibility for our own lives, we are more likely to take good care of ourselves. Although the medical profession may help us to do this, our bodies and minds are not their responsibility. Only we can take proper care of them.

I recently had reason to go to a physiotherapist for a bad back. He examined me and then told me that he could ease my present problem but the ongoing state of my back was, in fact, my responsibility. He then spent time showing me how to live in such a way as to take the stress off my back. It would be easy to find things or people to blame for its condition, but that would not make it better. Taking responsibility and following the physiotherapist's advice should.

Taking such responsibility not only encourages physical, mental and emotional health but also spiritual well-being. A person who is taking proper responsibility for his feelings, thoughts and actions is in a position to ask for and receive forgiveness from God and others when that is needed. Such a person can also forgive others when that is appropriate. C.S. Lewis paints a horrific picture of Hell in *The Great Divorce*. At one point he is in conversation with a man at the bus stop waiting for the bus to take them up to the 'High Countries'. This man knew two men who had been to see where Napoleon lived and they had actually seen the great man through one of the windows of his palace. Lewis is interested to hear what he was doing. Apparently the two men had watched him for about a year and all that time he just walked up and down, up and down, left-right, left-right. He never stopped for a moment. All the time he was muttering to himself: '"It was Soult's fault. It was Ney's fault. It was Josephine's fault. It was the fault of the Russians. It was the fault of the English." He never stopped for a moment. A little, fat man who looked sort of tired. But he didn't seem able to stop it.'[6] In the preface to *The Great Divorce*, Lewis writes: 'If we insist on keeping Hell (or even earth) we shall not see Heaven: if we accept Heaven we shall not be able to retain even the smallest and most intimate souvenirs of Hell.'[7]

The prodigal son took the full responsibility for his sin and by so doing came back into a relationship with his father. He was then able to regain his spiritual, emotional and physical health.

Encouraging the development of this discipline

Understanding what it means to take responsibility is not enough to spur us on in its use. We need to make a conscious decision or commitment to exercise it.

By using the first person singular more often

A helpful exercise for those who think they may not be employing the discipline sufficiently is to begin starting sentences with the first person singular. This is a way of owning feelings, thoughts and actions. Instead of saying, 'You made me angry when you did that,' you would say, 'I felt angry when you did that.' Or instead of saying, 'She made me buy that cake,' you would say, 'I made a mistake when I bought that cake.'

By admitting to inadequacy and inner emptiness

The truth is that we are all deficient, inadequate and sinful people. We are unable to help or to save ourselves, let alone others. The defensive position of shielding ourselves from facing this truth will only succeed in binding us into a non-growth situation. 'The Christian is one who has admitted his own hunger and thirst for right-relatedness to the sources of being and well-being. He does not share the common human illusion that it is disgraceful not to be able to cover up one's own deficiencies.'[8] Once he has admitted to his inner emptiness and powerlessness, the Christian is in a position to receive help both from God and from others.

By viewing the past in the light of our responsibility

Although many of our problems may have been caused in the first place by poor and thoughtless parenting, each one of us chose to react in different ways to that parenting. Once we have grieved over that which we failed to receive we must then take responsibility for our reactions and we must repent for those unhealthy and ungodly 'survival kits' we adopted. We need to look especially at those we have used continuously right up to the present time. So often, in counselling, a person begins to unlock the doors to his past history and then gets stuck in blaming others, or himself, for everything. He takes on the identity of 'the victim'. We need to ask the Spirit of Truth to illumine our past history so that we can recognise the part we in fact played in it and take responsibility for that.

By believing what the Bible says about sin

It is a natural and normal instinct to feel sin needs to be punished. If others sin against us we often make the mistake of wanting to punish them. But God reserves the right to be the Judge and He has already judged and punished all man's sin by sending His own Son to die. In His body Jesus took the judgment and the punishment that originally belonged to us (1 Pet.2:21–5). By blaming others we judge them and by continuing to do so we punish them. '"It is mine to avenge; I will repay," says the Lord' (Rom.12:19).

When we sin there are two ways of avoiding taking proper responsibility. One is to take up a big stick and punish ourselves unmercifully instead of repenting and appropriating the forgiveness God offers to us, as the responsible way of dealing with sin. Another avoidance mechanism is a bland reaction to personal sin. Instead of viewing sin from God's perspective we ignore the seriousness of what we have done. This is a way of apparently taking responsibility and yet avoiding the full weight. Repentance, which leads to salvation, only comes when we first take full responsibility for what we have done and cry out to God for mercy.

By deliberately taking up responsibility daily

Stuck to the mirror over his sink John Powell has a notice that confronts him every day: 'You are looking at the face of the person who is responsible for your happiness.'[9] Each of us needs intentionally and deliberately to take up responsibility for the day ahead. Perhaps the day will be shared with others, but responsibility for the day belongs to us.

John Powell suggests that there is something within each of us which affects our attitudes and view of reality. It is this that determines our emotional and behavioural reactions. Something within us makes life sad or glad, a success or a failure. Once a person acknowledges this and takes responsibility for his reactions and actions, he will enter into the fullness of life which is his legacy from God.

This was the experience of the prodigal son. As soon as he took responsibility he had begun the journey back to 'fullness of life' – back to his father. However, ahead of him lay a long, painful journey and only by practising our next discipline was he able to complete the journey.

Exercises

1. The following are clues to help you detect whether or not you are taking proper responsibility:
Do you rationalise your problems and difficulties away?
Do you make heavy weather of problems?
Do you feel responsible for other people's happiness?
Do you fear criticism?
Do you have a tendency to gloss over difficulties?
Do you attempt to punish those who hurt you?
Do you have a need to justify yourself when criticised?
Are you defensive when corrected?

Do you find it hard to receive forgiveness from God and others?

Do you often consider it your fault when something goes wrong?

Does your happiness depend on others?

If you scored six or more affirmatives you may have a problem taking proper responsibility.

2. Which side of the responsibility line do you come — taking too much or too little? Spend some time asking God to show you if there is anything in your childhood that would account for this.

3. Take it in turns to recount an incident when you have felt very angry. Start by saying, 'So and so made me very angry when . . .' Then try again and this time say it in a way that makes you responsible for your feelings.

4. Do you have a present difficulty in your life which you feel is caused by another person, past or present?

In front of your group/friend (or if alone, in your journal) try taking responsibility for the problem and for finding a solution to it. Tell your group/friend the solution that comes to mind. If this is difficult ask the group/friend to pray with you.

5. Do you feel able to agree with the last quotation in this chapter? If so, are there any changes you need to make in your attitudes, actions or reactions so that you can enjoy a greater fullness of life?

5. COMMITMENT TO THE PROCESS OF GROWTH

' "I will . . . go back to my father . . ." So he got
up and went to his father' (Luke 15:18,20).

The prodigal son made a decision to go home. Then he acted
upon that decision. We know that he eventually arrived
home, although we don't know how long the journey took
him nor what particular difficulties he encountered along
the way. Such details must be left to the imagination. He
might possibly have collapsed from time to time through
hunger and exhaustion but his earlier resolution to go home
propelled him towards his ultimate goal.

Only a daily commitment to the process of growth will
keep us on the road to maturity. It is an indispensable
discipline. Therefore we need to know what it entails.

An admission

First it is a recognition that the place you are in is not a
healthy or mature one. It is neither where you wish to be,
nor where you ought to be. The prodigal recognised his state
and admitted he was starving. There has to be a similar
honest admission in anyone before any real change can take
place in his life.

It is admitting that we are on a journey — a journey of
growth in God and into completeness in God but we are

not there yet. We have not reached *teleios*, which is rather misleadingly translated as 'perfect' in most versions of Matthew's Gospel. However, when we are enjoined to 'be perfect as your heavenly Father is perfect', it is not in the sense of moral perfection or total lack of imperfection. We are called to be *teleios* in the sense of being mature, full-grown, adult, complete. It is part of maturity to accept and own that we have quite a way to go towards completeness.[1]

I once talked with a young man at a conference who had had a very bad relationship with his father and consequently had never had his masculinity affirmed. He was stuck in an immature position battling with homosexual desires and fantasies. He asked for prayer for this. As we bowed our heads to pray he admitted his situation aloud to God, telling Him he wanted to be healed. In the midst of his prayers he began to groan painfully in desperation. With the audible admission and then the groans I felt a sense of hope rising within me that he was taking the first real step on the long journey towards wholeness.

An assessment

The prodigal made an assessment of his situation. 'How many of my father's hired men have food to spare, and here I am starving to death!' Perhaps home had been a little boring but at least there was ample provision of things to eat. He reckoned that he was not worthy to be a son, but possibly he could be taken back as a hired hand. He weighed up the probabilities.

Jesus warns us against starting to build without first counting the cost, or going to war without first calculating the chances of winning (Luke 14:28–33). Before committing to growth we each need to make a realistic assessment of our present position and the strength of our desire to change.

We also need to have some understanding of what the journey could involve. The people most likely to fall by the wayside are usually those whose condition at the start of the journey is poor. They may need a lot of emotional and spiritual build-up before they can even start along the road.

Jenny became a Christian after the break-up of her marriage. She had been born into a very dysfunctional family and this had caused her to develop unhealthy behaviour patterns. She had a life history of many wrong choices. Before she could realistically start the uphill climb to maturity she needed help to resolve some of these past issues. Without doing that she would never have coped with the journey at all. Too much extra luggage would have weighed her down and hindered her progress.

Others are both fit and healthy and capable of the journey but have not reckoned on the narrowness of the road. It then comes as a shock to realise how much has to be laid aside if the journey is to be pursued.

Once we have looked fairly and squarely at the condition of our hearts and have recognised and admitted its unhealthy state, then we must assess the situation. 'Do I really want to change?' 'Can I cope with the hard work involved, the pain and the uncovering before God and others?' 'Am I ready to make such a commitment?' Having assessed the situation we need to move on to the next stage.

An active decision

I have already mentioned the 'Communion in Marriage' course which our church runs each year, and it is only one of a number of different courses, each dealing with various problems and encouraging maturity in the lives of individuals, couples and families. Many people show interest in these courses. They may even say they're just what they need. However, what sometimes happens is that after a course has begun someone will tell me about a difficulty they have. When I ask them why they are not on the appropriate course, they say that they had really meant to attend but had never got around to signing up.

A decision only fully becomes commitment when action is taken to implement the decision. The desire to move from one position to another is an important step in commitment to growth but it will never happen unless the will is able to carry through the desire. We can wish for growth, hope for growth, imagine growth, but only a full commitment, that wills to grow, can achieve its objective.

To remain in a static place, blocked by our past hurts, our sin, our shame or our fear of change, is a refusal to grow. Gregory of Nyssa was reported to have said, 'Ultimately sin is a refusal to grow.'[2] God's purpose for His children is growth. He speaks again and again through Paul about growth and maturity. He warned the Colossian Christians against getting side-tracked and so disqualified from the prize. Such a person 'has lost connection with the Head, from whom the whole body, supported and held together by its ligaments and sinews, *grows as God causes it to grow*' (Col.2:19).

Jesus asked the man at the pool of Bethesda, 'Do you want to get well?' Or as it says in the Authorised Version, 'Wilt thou be made whole?' Jesus encouraged him to exercise his freedom of choice and will to be whole. According to Charles Kraft, our wills are the most important factor in any changes that we make. 'Will is undoubtedly the most important factor in a change of perspective. There are at least three points in the process where the way we exercise our wills is crucial. (a) We either will to be open to a change or to be closed to it. Then, even if we open up to the possibility, (b), we either will to make the change or not. If we do decide to make the change, (c), we either will to continue with our decision or eventually give up.'[3]

Although God has given each of us the gift of free will, it would appear from Scripture that the will of man can become weakened or disabled in some way. Because of the importance of the will in healing we examine the will in more detail in a further chapter.

The importance of commitment to growth

Why is a commitment to growth an important discipline? Because a commitment is more than a good idea! It is an 'obligation, a promise, an engagement: a declared attachment to a doctrine or a cause' (Chamber's *Everyday Dictionary*).

A promise or an obligation carries weight. An engagement is not broken lightly. Therefore a commitment to something increases the likelihood that it will, eventually, be fulfilled even when there are difficulties and other things that may seem at times to be more attractive. At eighteen I was living in digs in Oxford and enjoying a completely godless and selfish existence. One day I was handed a formally printed invitation card by a fellow lodger. It was for a guest service at her church the following week. By the wording I presumed this was a personal invitation to me and I therefore had to give a definite reply. So I made a commitment to go with her. When the next Sunday came I was asked by a close friend to go with her to the cinema to see one of my favourite film stars. The only reason that stopped me opting out of the church service and accepting what seemed the more attractive invitation was the fact that I had already made a promise to my fellow lodger. That Sunday evening I became a Christian.

When a commitment has been made a person is more likely to keep going even when the progress is slow or hard or when occasionally it becomes completely blocked. The point at which this commitment becomes vital is when subtle and seductive distractions come along to waylay and deter a person from attaining his determined goal.

Diversions

In the process of growth some diversions are particularly common.

The temptation to blame-shift and self-pity

Understanding and knowing our personal history can be an important part of the healing process. This in turn facilitates growth. As already mentioned, when the pain of past hurts is uncovered some people can spiral temporarily into blaming those who were responsible for their hurt. This is fairly normal and natural. However, too long a stay in the place of blaming is unhealthy. Self-pity follows inevitably and then one is locked into a descending path which is weakening and destructive. It leads nowhere and resolves nothing. Just a short while ago I was saddened to hear a woman of thirty still identifying with the abused child of the past. Even after hours of ministry she could not bring herself to drop the pernicious activity of blame-shifting and self-pity.

Healthy grieving, on the other hand, is a healing process. Instead of a few superficial, self-pitying tears, a deep, cleansing grief is expressed, followed by an experience of healing and restoration. In the process some anger is often ventilated as part of the grief work, but it is unusual for such a person to stay angry for too long. Normally forgiveness flows easily out of such an experience.

I remember praying with a young girl whose extremely critical father was a controlling influence in her life. Although she had a responsible job and was quite self-sufficient in other ways, she felt unnaturally dominated by her father. During the prayer time with her we asked her what she was feeling. She said she felt very angry with her father. As she said this she began to beat her fists on her knees and shout at her father as if he were present. After a while the anger turned into tears for the loss of her very affirming mother. We were about to encourage her to forgive her father when she began again to express anger towards him, shouting at him to get off her back. She had still not emptied out the pool of rage completely. But gradually the feelings subsided and then she was able to release forgiveness quite easily. When she opened her eyes she looked as if she had resolved a major issue in her life. There was no longer any hint of blame towards her father. She still needed, however, to let him know that she was now an adult and therefore did not want him to control her life any more, but she felt able to do this lovingly.

The problem of emotional dependency

Over-dependency on other people has already been mentioned as a common method of survival for some emotionally damaged people. When someone who has lacked sufficient nurture in his early years makes a close relationship, whether in friendship or in counselling, he will be tempted to have his immature attachment-needs met in the relationship. At this point he may well lose sight of the journey to maturity he was in the process of making. The feelings of being loved, of being cared for, of knowing someone is there just for him, are so intoxicating for a person with a 'deprived child' still inside him, that he can easily deceive himself and begin to use the old 'survival kit' once again.

In *The Healing Presence*, Leanne Payne includes a prayer for the healing of the will. In that prayer is a request that God will reveal any way in which we are 'bent toward the creature' (a term she uses to denote those who are looking to others for something only God can give them):

Show me any way in which I am bent toward the creature; O Lord, reveal any idolatrous or neurotic dependency on persons or things, show me any way in which I demand from the created the identity I can gain only from You, my Creator.

She then encourages the reader to visualise any bentness the Lord may be showing them and then to see themselves deliberately straightening up from that idol and praying:

I choose, Lord, to forsake this bentness, I confess it to you, just now, as the sin that it is, I renounce it in Your name, and I thank You for Your forgiveness, I receive it.[4]

Some degree of dependency is normal in a counselling situation, or in a close friendship, but when the relationship becomes an all-consuming and exclusive passion it has become unhealthy. This sort of dependency needs to be renounced, as in the above prayer, and a re-commitment to the process of maturity made.

The seduction of self-analysis

Self-analysis can become a seductive attraction. The focus on inner-healing and prayer counselling has caused many Christian leaders to be concerned about narcissistic implications, the interest this can generate in the self. 'We must focus on Christ and not on ourselves,' they say. However, a Christian who struggles with problems and difficulties which no amount of private prayer and self-effort has apparently shifted obviously needs some outside help. The aim of ministry to such a person is to deal as effectively as possible with the problem so that the journey to maturity may continue unhindered. Once a person has decided to open himself to healing some investigation of the past is necessary. However, when this becomes an unhealthy introspection it is dangerous. Analysing and dissecting past and present problems can become so engrossing that the goal of maturity is temporarily obscured.

A person who falls into introspection is usually focusing on the false-self with all its intricate survival mechanisms, rather than opening up the inner, damaged self to Jesus for healing. He is focusing on the thoughts, feelings and behaviour patterns which belong to the 'survival kit'. In fact the only attention this fleshly contrivance needs is whatever effort and energy it takes to dismantle it. The deadly narcissistic disease of introspection tends to give it so much attention that it grows in strength. The 'false-self' needs to be crucified not actualised by too much attention.

> In spite of self-preoccupation, most people do not truly know themselves. Their focus has been not their true selves but their hurts, and anxieties and their false selves, the selves they think themselves to be. They cannot give them up until they see them as false selves. In other words, they cannot transcend self until they move past the various false selves that are their preoccupations and block them from real life. Then, coming to see their true selves they are able to understand their need to surrender to God.[5]

The delusion of self-fulfilment

The lure of self-fulfilment is another subtle temptation which Satan uses to put the eyes on self and off Christ. Many of the modern psychotherapies focus a group's attention on self-fulfilling and self-actualising techniques. It is very easy to become mesmerised and enthralled by discoveries about oneself. My individual thought. . . processes and responses can be fascinating! The objectives of self-fulfilment and self-actualisation are not Christian objectives. God's sole purpose for a Christian is that he/she be transformed into the image of Christ. Although some of the techniques used in secular psychotherapy can be useful in learning to recognise one's own survival mechanisms and the way in which they actually block one's personal growth, fallen man will always need to guard against self-enthronement. Jesus taught that 'If anyone would come after me, he must deny himself and take up his cross daily and follow me. For whoever wants to save his life will lose it, but whoever loses his life for me will save it' (Luke 9:23,24).

Tiredness and discouragement

It should be fully understood that growth is a process. Without such understanding it is easy to become discouraged. It is not going to be attained in one quick step. It will be a long-term process with various stages to it. In my own life I have sometimes dealt quickly with a particular problem and have then felt discouraged if several years later I seem to be struggling with the same difficulty, although in fact this has usually been from a different angle or at greater depth. It seems that just as the road to maturity is apparently becoming more effortless and easy to negotiate, we round a bend and find ourselves in rugged terrain again and have to use all our energy to keep going.

Recently a friend confided in me that God had been refining her in an uncomfortable way during the past year and she hoped it was now over. A few months later when the new year had only just begun she found herself struggling with the same problems of the previous year. At first she was extremely discouraged and for a while looked as if she would sink into a pit of despair. This could have trapped her and held up the work God was accomplishing within her. Fortunately, her commitment to growth was a strong one so she put her head down against the storm and pressed on, accepting that God could use the trial to make some necessary changes in her life.

The inadequacy of short-term goals

Occasionally a person's commitment is solely towards

solving the immediate problem. The present difficulty may be resolved for a while but unless there is a long-term goal of maturity the problem, or a similar one, could return. For this reason to make maturity one's aim is so much more beneficial, as well as being God's will for us.

A young man came to us seeking help for a relationship problem. It was soon apparent that his way of relating was very immature. I suggested that we work together to help that emotionally stunted part of him to mature. If he set his heart on growing-up I was sure he would then find the present difficulty, and any future ones, easier to handle. At first he did not want to accept the long-term solution and the work it might involve. He was all for dealing with the present difficulty as quickly as possible, however painful, with the hope that it would never return to bother him again. I agreed that the present difficulty had to be resolved but the long-term objective of growth would be of greater value to him.

Short-term goals are quite acceptable, providing they are seen in terms of steps to growth. In other words someone may have a pressing problem and seek help to resolve it. If this person is seriously working at growth in his life on a daily basis, then asking for help to resolve an immediate problem is a step in that growth process.

The deceit of unworthy goals

There are some aspirations which could be part of a desire for maturity or simply an extension of the old 'survival kit'. For example, the aim to be part of the ministry team of a church may be a desire to grow in serving others. However it could also be a way of boosting a low self-image and minimising the bad feelings of being worthless. The desire to go back to college and get another degree could be part of growth and maturity, but the motivation could equally be a feeling of inadequacy and uselessness when comparing oneself with others. We must learn to recognise when we are motivated by the flesh and the hurts and pain of the past.

One of C.S. Lewis's Angels in *The Great Divorce* invites a very cultured and religious Ghost to accompany him on the long, arduous journey to the mountains (Heaven). He explains that the journey may be painful at first. The Ghost appears ready to consider the invitation but insists on being given some guarantees first. He is only prepared to consider a place where he will find a wider sphere of usefulness – and scope for the talents that God has given him. Also he requires an atmosphere of free enquiry – in fact all that he means by civilisation and the spiritual life.

The Angel refuses to promise the Ghost any of these things. He cannot be given a sphere of usefulness because he is not needed there at all. No scope for his talents: only forgiveness for having perverted them. No atmosphere of enquiry, because he will be going to a land not of questions but of answers and a place where he would see the face of God.

This poor, religious Ghost seemed unimpressed by the promise of being taken into the presence of Almighty God. Instead he continued to be caught up in trivialities. Eventually the Angel turns away, leaving the Ghost to his own devices. He had had the chance to make the most incredible journey of his life and had chosen instead to be side-tracked by the relatively unworthy pursuit of intellectualism.[6]

After Paul states his goal of knowing Christ and becoming like Him in his death, he goes on to say:

Not that I have already obtained all this, or have already been made perfect, but I press on to take hold of that for which Christ Jesus took hold of me. Brothers, I do not consider myself yet to have taken hold of it. But one thing I do: Forgetting what is behind and straining towards what is ahead, I press on towards the goal to win the prize for which God has called me heavenwards in Christ Jesus (Phil.3:12–14).

Let us, then commit ourselves to our goal and, like Paul, 'press on' until we achieve it.

Exercises

1. Where are you in the growth process?
   Have you begun?
   Have you begun and plateaued?
   Did you begin well and now feel blocked?
   Make an honest assessment of your position and share it with the group/friend/journal.

2. If you feel ready to do so make a verbal commitment to start or continue in the growth process. Do this by first saying where you see yourself now and then where you would like to be.

3. Did you identify with any of the diversions mentioned in the chapter? Take a few minutes to let God search your hearts.

   Are you in any way dependent on another person to meet your needs for security or self-worth? 'Are you bent towards the creature?' – as Leanne Payne describes it. Use the pattern outlined on pages 67 and 68 to help you – the prayer, the visualisation and the renunciation.

   This pattern can be used for any of the other diversions you feel either in danger of making or have already made.

4. Share your findings with your group/friend/journal. Any prayer of renunciation is always best made aloud with others present.

6. THE WILL

' "I will set out . . ." So he got up and went . . .'
(Luke 15:18,20)

The prodigal made a decision to return home. Having verbally articulated it he then took a positive step to bring about the desired change in his life.

The will plays an important part in the process of change and growth. We have the God-given ability to make choices. This ability includes the possibility of making wrong choices; choices that can be harmful and destructive to ourselves and to other people. The will is not naturally directed towards loving and serving God. We are daily confronted with choices about whether to serve ourselves or to serve God. We have the choice to be selfish or self-less; to be wilful or willing; to live to self or die to self; to be rebellious or to be subject to God.

Some people naturally have very strong wills. These may be directed towards God or towards the self. Whichever they choose to serve they do it with determination and energy. Others, however, seem to possess little strength of will. It would seem from the Bible and from observation that the will can fall into various states of disrepair. It's helpful to look at some of the different conditions of the will and how it could be strengthened. John Bradshaw in his book, *The Family*, writes of our will becoming disabled. 'Our will is the executor of our life and the core of our freedom. Our will becomes disabled because it loses its eyes as it were . . .'

Our reasoning, judgments and perceptions become biased through blocked emotions. It is as if the will becomes blind and it can no longer see what it is doing. Bradshaw continues: 'We become blindly wilful. I believed for years,' he says, 'that I could stop drinking any time I really wanted to. I pointed to my times of abstinence as proof of this. The fact was I could stop. But what I couldn't do was stay stopped.'[1]

Most people agree with the concept of change and growth but some seem unable to bring themselves to the point of making the necessary commitment for starting the process. Some may even reach the point of committing to change but according to the state of their wills the journey may be either extremely difficult, relatively straightforward or never actually begun. God's amazing gift of free will − the power to choose − seems to fall victim to a variety of ills.

Different states of the will

The weak will (2 Tim.3:6)

Someone with a weak will is easily influenced by other people and finds it hard to be sure of his own opinions. He rarely makes choices based on truth and reality but more often on feelings and the excitement of the moment. New Year's resolutions are made and broken with a shrug, as if to say, 'Well that's the way I am.'

Two ladies I know of similar age became Christians at about the same time. Both were attractive, vivacious women and were quickly caught up in the excitement of having a new direction to their lives, making new friends and being involved in new activities. Gradually, however, the initial excitement began to wane. Each was faced with committing to the everyday work of discipleship. One of the ladies fixed her eyes on Jesus and began a steady journey forward with

Christ. The other, sadly weak willed, could not maintain the commitment. When something which she found more exciting came along off she dashed. She is now in the far country.

The captive will (2 Tim.2:26)

A free will was originally God's gift to us. It is still His desire for us to freely choose to love and serve Him. For some it seems especially difficult to choose to go God's way. To some degree their wills appear to be in bondage to Satan. This means the choices they make are destructive and unhealthy ones, both for themselves and often for those near to them in their family, in their church and in their work place. They may agree in principle that God's ways are best but they seem unable to make that choice when the moment comes.

Severe depression can also paralyse the will to the extent that the sufferer seems unable to make healthy choices. Recently I was called out of a Sunday service to pray for a young man who was so depressed that he wanted to end his life. He had been diagnosed as having clinical depression. As I sat silently beside him I wondered how best to help him. Then I remembered Agnes Sanford who said, 'The depressed mind is the sick mind, always. And the sick mind cannot unlock its own doors to the healing peace of God.'[2] Bearing this in mind, I told him to just sit still while I prayed for him. He seemed unable to pray for himself or to choose to get well. I believe the prayers said for him that night kept him from suicide. He was admitted to hospital the next day and has since begun a gradual recovery.

The resistant will (Rom.9:19)

Paul puts this in the form of a question: 'Who resists his will?' The answer, of course, is that everyone does and

Christians are included amongst them. Often a Christian is resistant to God's will because of fear and mistrust. God is misconceived as being harsh and distant and untrustworthy. These people distort the character of God by transferring onto Him their feelings towards past authority figures. They may theoretically accept the truth of God's love but because there has, as yet, been no healing of the inner-self their negative feelings still control them.

A resistant will may be a rebellious will, filled not with fear but with anger towards God. God is accused of being the cause of all the abuse and hurt they have received. Before anger can be properly laid down its true origin needs to be recognised and confronted. Anger is a secondary emotion. Beneath the anger there lies a great deal of pain. The hurt may have been inflicted unintentionally but it still needs to be laid bare. Once the real source of the hurt is uncovered, God can then begin the healing process. Forgiveness needs to be released to those who consciously or unconsciously inflicted the hurt. Anger diverted towards God and away from the real cause may block a person's growth indefinitely.

The controlled will (1 Cor.7:37)

A man who can control his passions in the way Paul is suggesting here is a person with a great deal of inner strength and his will is well controlled. In this instance Paul is obviously commending self-control, which is one of the fruits of the Spirit. Occasionally, however, a person with a very controlled will may be overly controlling his feelings by suppression which can be detrimental to health. In such a case there is probably an underlying fear of losing control. This sort of person often has a need to control life generally. He tries to control his situation and those around him, which means he would rather lead than be led and will keep everything firmly in his own hands. In that way he can be sure of keeping control. This need to control and dominate indicates a deep insecurity. Often instead of being willing to look at the root cause of his need to control, the 'controller' determines only to keep his 'survival kit' in place. Instead of committing himself to healing he commits himself to minimising any inner discomfort by over-controlling.

Andrew is a middle-aged man who appears on the surface to be very calm and efficient, although rather wooden, perhaps. In reality he is an extremely angry man who dominates and controls those he lives with by his hostile presence. Andrew's father had a violent temper and the whole family had lived in fear of his rages. When Andrew discovered that, like his father, he was prone to violent outbursts he chose to control his anger by becoming distant from others and suppressing all his feelings. Those who live with him are afraid of what lies underneath his excessive self-control. They suspect devastating consequences if the control were to snap. On several occasions Andrew has been given the opportunity to uncover and look at his difficult feelings but his will is still on the side of suppression and not growth.

The eager will (2 Cor.8:11)

In this instance Paul was commending the Corinthians for their initial enthusiasm. They had eagerly agreed to be generous. 'Now,' Paul wrote, 'finish the work, so that your eager willingness to do it may be matched by your completion of it, according to your means.' What he was saying is: 'Put your feet where your mouth is!' An eager or enthusiastic will sometimes promises more than it can give and has to be balanced by reality. 'Don't promise a hundred pounds when in fact you only have fifty to give. Be realistic about your commitment.'

The over-eager person may be more interested in quick, rather dramatic solutions than the daily, mundane work of growth. He enthusiastically embraces healing at a conference but the eagerness fades later when he then finds he still has to face the out-working of that healing.

A reluctant will (Matt.23:37)

Jesus longed to gather the people of Jerusalem to Himself as a hen would gather her chicks beneath her wings to protect them. But Jerusalem was unwilling: her inhabitants were reluctant to turn to Christ for any help. We usually do this only as a last resort. This was how it was with the prodigal who eventually 'came to his senses' (Luke 15:17) and realised that his father and his father's house was still there. The option of returning home did not appeal to him until he had reached desperation point.

A person who is unwilling to seek God's help with his problems may easily opt for shortcut answers which fail to reach the root of the problem. A superficial commitment to God baulks at exerting any real effort. We once prayed for a young woman who had a compulsion to meet her need for affirmation with an ungodly 'quick-fix'. She craved the praises of others and because she was a gifted performer she was able to feed her addiction. She found it hard to ever delay gratification in this area. On one occasion she agreed to spend some time with a few friends seeking God and asking Him to meet this deep inner need. Soon after this arrangement was made she was invited to perform at a special function. Her previous commitment was instantly forgotten in the excitement of another 'quick-fix'. Her reluctance to give up her habitual 'survival kit' meant that she lost an opportunity for finding a godly way of meeting the deep need within her.

The rich young ruler was given a similar choice. He was reluctant to take the risk of giving up his great wealth to follow Jesus. We are told 'he went away sad' (Mark 10:22). A Christian with a reluctant will often falters in his discipleship when faced with the choice between an old way of living and a more godly way.

If exercising our will is such an important part of our commitment to growth, how can we strengthen or redirect it?

The healing of the will

Paul exhorted the Philippians to 'work out your salvation with fear and trembling [their part], for, 'it is God who works in you to will and to act according to his good purpose [God's part]' (Phil.2:12,13).

Doubtless the prodigal began that arduous journey home in fear and trepidation. Then we read, 'But while he was still a long way off, his father saw him and was filled with compassion for him; he ran to his son, threw his arms around him and kissed him' (Luke 15:20). Possibly the father even carried his exhausted son the last lap of the journey home. Once we have made the commitment God will come to meet us and help us but there are also things we must do to help ourselves. We must strengthen our feeble arms and weak knees! We must make level paths for our feet, 'so that the lame may not be disabled, but rather healed' (Heb.12:12,13).

There are various means by which the will can be strengthened and the path to maturity made easier.

By prayer

The first and most vital way of healing the will is to pray for it, both on one's own and with others. Before beginning to minister to a person with emotional problems it would be wise to discover the state of that person's will. Ask him what sort of choices he has made in the past, and how difficult he finds it in the present to choose God's way. Then begin the ministry by praying for the will to be strengthened and directed towards God and His purposes for his life. Leanne Payne emphasises the need for this type of prayer, especially in cases where the will has been bound for a long time. This means that the will is not only passive but is also undeveloped and withered. She suggests praying for its freedom and strengthening, even for an outright miracle of restoration.

> I pray, Lord, for the release and strengthening of my will, that creative, masculine part of me, that with which I initiate change, choose life, and with which I forsake the bent, idolatrous position of attempting to find my identity in the creature.[3]

Continued prayer is needed to ensure Satan does not once again ensnare the will.

By exercise

The will needs to be strengthened not only by prayer but by exercise, particularly if it is weak. A man with a heart weakened by stress and his body affected by bad diet should not sit and do nothing, hoping his heart will get strengthened by itself and his body slimmed on its own. He should alter his diet and begin a little exercise, increasing it gradually until his body gets fit and his heart muscles have increased their capacity and can cope with normal life. In the same way a weak will should be activated and stretched. Immediately a person has received prayer for his will he should be encouraged to choose God and His will instead of self and obedience to self's demands. If he has been avoiding dealing with a certain problem to do with work, for example, he should be encouraged to choose there and then to confront the difficulty as soon as possible.

Many people have a problem resolving conflict in their

relationships. One woman came to see us after she had been
put in a position of leadership. She found herself avoiding
conflict with those under her and consequently bad feelings
were beginning to smoulder all around. Her will to resolve
such issues seemed bound by her fear of becoming
unpopular. With encouragement and prayer she gradually
began to make some new choices. Little by little she tried
to confront the different problems. Finally she came to a
place where she had to articulate her position as leader out
loud to the others. This was something she would normally
have been incapable of doing. However, her will had grown
stronger and although she had to listen to the group express
some bad feelings she stuck to her position. She was both
amazed and delighted when the conflict was resolved and
peace restored.

By changing diet

A man with a weak heart needs exercise but probably he
also needs to change his diet. Because most of us have chosen
to meet our needs or minimise our inner discomfort in selfish
and unhealthy ways, our wills have become disabled and
weak. As with the prodigal son, the will has been directed
towards satisfying the carnal nature. Now we have to 'put
that off' and direct our wills toward all that is godly. 'You
were taught, with regard to your former way of life, to put
off your old self, which is being corrupted by its deceitful
desires; to be made new in the attitude of your minds; and
to put on the new self, created to be like God in true
righteousness and holiness' (Eph.4:22–4).

The Philippian Christians were exhorted to make sure
their diet for the inner man was good. 'Finally, brothers,
whatever is true, whatever is noble, whatever is right,
whatever is pure, whatever is lovely, whatever is admirable
– if anything is excellent or praiseworthy – think about
such things' (Phil.4:8). This meant that the mind was to

focus on images of glory instead of images of destruction. This diet will invigorate and energise the will towards God. A diet which consists of too much unedifying material (junk food), will dissipate the will increasingly until it becomes captive by the prince of this world.

By changing the object of our vision

Until that moment of decision the prodigal son had been focusing on himself. First on his pleasure and then on his survival. Then he took his eyes off himself and pictured his father at home. These thoughts motivated him to take action.

The object of our commitment is a vital factor in our growth. The pursuit of self − self-protection, self-gratification, self-actualisation, self-fulfilment − can only lead, in the end, to disillusionment, soul sickness and, ultimately, death. Jesus said, 'What good is it for a man to gain the whole world, yet forfeit his soul?' (Mark 8:36). Once the prodigal son had his sights fixed on getting home he was motivated. Most likely he had to rest often. He may well have wondered if he would ever make it. In those moments I am sure he had nostalgic fantasies of home; the warmth of the log fire, the table laden with food and his father posed patiently before the mantelpiece.

The object of our commitment must be a worthy one; one that will keep us going even when it is hard. Paul's objective was to know Christ. 'I want to know Christ and the power of his resurrection and the fellowship of sharing in his sufferings, becoming like him in his death, and so, somehow, to attain to the resurrection from the dead' (Phil.3:10,11).

A will directed towards God is vital for healing and growth. When the disciples asked Jesus why He spoke to the people in parables He quoted Isaiah who said: 'You will be ever hearing but never understanding; you will be ever seeing but never perceiving. For this people's heart has become calloused; they hardly hear with their ears, and they have closed their eyes. Otherwise they might see with their eyes, hear with their ears, understand with their hearts and turn, and I would heal them' (Matt.13:14,15).

The choice to hear, the choice to see, the choice to understand is ours. The secrets of the Kingdom are plain to those who choose to turn to Christ and commit themselves to following Him. Let us pray for the will to do so.

We will need to remind ourselves often of this commitment to growth as we exercise the disciplines outlined. The next one may seem difficult for some people and there will need to be a willingness to take risks as the discipline is attempted.

Exercises

1. Do you identify with any of the states of will mentioned in this chapter?

2. Share with the group/friend/journal which description fits you the most. Illustrate this from your life if you can.

3. If you feel you are in need of healing of the will use the prayer on page 81. If you can, pray the prayer aloud and then ask the group to pray with you for the Holy Spirit's strengthening and healing of your will.

4. Spend some time helping each other find ways in which you could exercise your will during the next week.
For example:
Doing a cleaning or maintenance job in the house.
Writing a letter you have been putting off.
Contacting an acquaintance.
Making an apology.

Giving a gift.

Paying an outstanding debt.

5. Read Philippians, chapter four, verse eight, together and ask God to show you if there is anything in your daily lives which could cause your wills to be weakened or disabled. Share this with the group and look for ways of helping one another change.

6. Try honestly to evaluate the priorities in your life. To what do you give most of your time, energy, interest and money? This will be the thing in your life you most value.

Do you need to change the object of your vision?

How can you begin to do this? Share your intentions with your group/friend/journal.

7. COMMITMENT TO COMMUNICATE

' "I will set out and go back to my father and *say* to him: Father, I have sinned against heaven and against you. I am no longer worthy to be called your son . . ." The son *said* to him, "Father, I have sinned against heaven and against you. I am no longer worthy to be called your son" ' (Luke 15:18,19,21).

Having made his decision to return home, the prodigal son would no doubt have begun anticipating the first moments with his father. How should he cope with the situation? Should he arrive and say nothing; should he try and justify himself; should he be frank and open about how he felt? As we know he decided on the latter course. The result was a moving exchange which took place between the father and son as they became reconciled. It was true communication which brought them together again.

Of all the disciplines, communication might appear the least important. In some ways it is possible to change and grow without in-depth interaction with others. However, the speed and extent of the growth may be greatly affected. Without communication with others we are never likely to reach our full stature. Growth is greatly facilitated when we are able to share ourselves; our joys, our hopes, our disappointments, our frustrations and our difficulties, with at least one other person. John Powell suggests that unless we feel understood by at least one person we will not develop freely or find a full life. In order to see ourselves clearly we must be open to a chosen confidant who is worthy of our trust.[1]

True communication

Before examining the 'pros' and 'cons' of this discipline we need to be sure we understand it. Those who have never enjoyed in-depth communication may have very little idea of what it involves. Just because we all learned to talk as children does not mean we are adept at true communication. It is a complex activity and has many facets.

Sharing

Communication is a relational exercise. You cannot do it alone. When we communicate we share something of ourselves with other people. 'Through our acts of sharing or communication we know and we are known. You share the gift of yourself with me, and I share the gift of myself with you.'[2] In this sharing we allow at least one other person into our world and go with him into his. Although a very shy man, Dr Paul Tournier had the gift of relating deeply with other human beings. He wrote: 'In order to understand a man we must follow him into all the detailed places of his life as he describes them to us. We must relive them with him. Listening to such accounts, I have in imagination shared the lives of many, many people, in places that have become as personal to me as those of my own life, so that real human fellowship has grown between us.'[3]

Hard work

For some, this act of sharing is almost too hard and costly. The introverted, the shy, the secretive, the self-conscious person will find it particularly difficult − on all levels. That is not to say that the extroverted, friendly, talkative, unself-conscious person will find it easy to communicate at the feelings level. And this is the level at which growth occurs. To be committed to growth is to commit ourselves to improving our communication, and we must know at which point we are stuck in order for this improvement to take place.

Different levels

In his book, *Why Am I Afraid to Tell You Who I Am?*, John Powell sets out five different levels of communication. The first level is the *cliché or conversation level*. All of us employ this type of exchange most days of our life, i.e. 'How are you?' 'Isn't the weather terrible?' 'The money goes nowhere these days.' At this level there is no real sharing of oneself. No risks are taken. It is a safe, non-relational level.

The next level is *reporting facts*. Here slightly more effort is needed. Some thinking and listening takes place, i.e., 'A storm is on the way. Did you hear the news?' Or, 'Children are such a worry. How many do you have?'

Level three is *sharing opinions*. This is a little more risky. At this level there is a chance of being disagreed with or of one's views being criticised. However, it is still possible to avoid the pain of rejection. Opinions are just ideas formed through reading or hearing other people's views and can easily be changed. For example, to say to someone, 'I don't agree with divorce,' is to express an opinion which could be changed after hearing the other person's views on the subject.

The fourth level is *sharing feelings*. This is even less safe. In fact at this level many people may feel quite uncomfortable and vulnerable. By sharing their feelings they are exposing a much more real part of themselves. Feelings tell us more about the true person than do opinions. Feelings are unique to each individual. Many people feel that no one else could ever have felt exactly like they feel. The risk is that, having shared a feeling, the person with whom one has shared it will respond in a critical way and say, 'You shouldn't feel like that.' This would amount to a rejection. He would be saying: 'I don't accept you the way you are. You are unacceptable to me.' When John Powell was just finishing his book, *Why Am I Afraid to Tell You Who I Am?*, a lady came into his office and asked him what he was doing. When he told her the title of the book he had been writing, she asked him if he wanted an answer to his question. When he said that he did, she told him that she was afraid to tell him who she was because if she did he might not like who she was, and that was all she had.[4] To share a feeling is to tell another person who one really is. This involves the risk of being rejected.

The last level is *peak communication*. This is one of total honesty and openness and it is only achieved occasionally. In that rare moment a complete emotional and spiritual communion takes place. Because of the degree of acceptance, affirmation and rapport which occurs at this depth of relating, healing, growth and change are inevitable consequences.

Levels of communication

Cliché Conversation — 'Nice weather!'
Reporting Facts — 'The roads are very congested'
Sharing Opinions — 'I don't agree with abortion'
Sharing Feelings — 'I feel lonely'
Peak Communication — 'I am afraid of death'

The level of communication determines whether or not it is a growth experience.

Different ways

Besides different levels there are also different ways of communicating. A touch or a look can sometimes convey more than words and be more convincing as well. A short while ago I prayed with a lady who struggles with a fear of being rejected. As she tried, very nervously, to share her feelings with me I wanted to reassure her of my support and acceptance of her as a person, whatever she told me. Instead of using words which could have cut across her efforts to communicate I stretched out my arm and took her hand. It was clearly the right way of communicating at that moment. She clutched my hand tightly in return and began to pour out her deepest fears, trusting that I would not reject her.

A thoughtful gift or a written note can be an effective way of communicating love and appreciation. We are blessed to be living in a very supportive community. Frequently we find expressions of love and support through the letter box. On one occasion a lady rang the house and left a message asking me not to prepare supper that evening. Later a ready-to-eat roast appeared in tinfoil on the doorstep. The gift told me that that person not only cared but had understood the pressure I was under at the time. In another place we lived, whenever we returned from a trip away from home we would find a bar of our favourite chocolate under our pillow. It had been put there by the friend who always kept an eye on the house for us and it communicated to us her love and her joy at having us back again. For us these were very meaningful ways of communicating.

Whatever method is used, any communication that deepens our relationships will be important to our health and growth. When God made man He decided it was not good for man to be alone and made a helper suitable for him, (Gen.2:18). Before Jesus left His disciples He prayed for them. Amongst other things, He prayed that they would be one as He and His Father were one, (John 17:11). Jesus longed that they would experience the same richness and depth in their relationship with one another as He and His Father enjoyed with each other. However, there are certain circumstances which can prevent us from communicating meaningfully.

Hindrances to communication

Our culture

Personality has some bearing upon how much effort we have to make at communication. But more likely the environment in which one grows up will have a greater degree of influence. Our English culture has led us to believe that an 'English man's home is his castle'. We value independence and individualism highly. We may never come to question the possible ill effects resulting from these values. Our culture can sometimes mislead us into irrational and wrong assumptions about life. Often we have no real cause to doubt the validity of our beliefs until we are exposed to another nationality.

Our first year in South America was spent in culture shock! Of the many differences their way of relating and communicating was one of the most difficult for us to cope with. The 'bear hug' greeting, or *abrazo*, invaded our safety zones; their frank and direct way of asking questions or making personal comments often offended our English sensitivities. They did not prize privacy in the way that we did. When we entered their homes they would greet us with the words: '*Su Casa*' – 'Your house'. It cut right across our 'castle complex'. At every turn, our friendly, outgoing Chilean friends innocently challenged a life-time of accumulated cultural assumptions.

Our English culture, prizing independence and individualism, is doomed to loneliness. A recent article in the *Daily Telegraph* bears this out. It spoke of the contemporary family as a 'collection of individuals who just happen to share the same address . . . day-to-day communication consists more of hastily scribbled notes than face-to-face conversation . . . The average family unit finds little reason to talk nowadays. Talking to other members of one's immediate family requires time and effort today, and many people do not appear to have either commodity.'[5]

A person who has been brought up in an environment of non-communication will find the discipline of communication at any deep level hard to put into practice. Just as our culture and our individual environment exert a strong influence, so too will past experiences of communicating — both the positive and the negative ones.

Past experience of communication

To share a feeling with a friend, to be listened to fully and taken seriously, is very reassuring. Equally to be rejected, after communicating something as personal as a feeling, can be devastating.

Childhood experiences exert a strong influence. Some past rejection may have initiated a reaction of fear so that when a person is about to disclose his real feelings the fear of rejection overwhelms any desire to communicate. In a counselling situation a counsellee will often hesitatingly start to say something and then break off saying, 'Oh nothing; it doesn't matter.' Even though the counsellor may encourage the person to share, the fear of rejection is so strong that he seems unable to open up. He only shakes his head in silent despair.

A separation anxiety may also be a block to effective sharing. This creates a warning system which says: 'Don't get too close or you will be hurt when they leave you.' The fear of the inevitable separation, inevitable only in the sufferer's mind, prevents any intimacy from occurring.

In the same way a commitment anxiety can prevent a person from meaningful communication. This fear says: 'If I get close I will be engulfed, swallowed up and will lose my own identity.' These irrational fears go back to bad past experiences of intimacy, probably in very early childhood. Part of the healing will come through prayer and part will come by pushing, little by little, through the fear barrier until increasing intimacy with one or two 'safe' people is established.

The benefits of gut-level communication

Communication is hard work for some and holds irrational fears for others, but the benefits should be enough to encourage anyone to persevere.

It encourages maturity

When we communicate our feelings, we bring them into the light where examination is possible. Immature or irrational reactions can be recognised, perhaps for the first time; change then becomes a possibility. If the feeling is shared with someone who values our growth, then further in-depth examination may follow. Take the case of a young man who shared his thoughts with a friend about changing his job. The friend asked him how he felt about it. He replied by articulating his thoughts again. But the friend insisted on knowing what he felt about it. Eventually he opened up and shared his fear of failure and what failure did to him. He said that his worth and value seemed to be based upon whether or not he succeeded; he felt unacceptable when he failed to meet the standard he had set for himself. This sort

of exchange helps us to clarify the unconscious drives and
motives behind our actions. It puts us in the position of being
able to make mature choices based on reality. It is often
difficult to arrive at this position on our own.

It increases emotional and mental health

One of our small grandsons was able to tell his mother of
his unhappiness at school. He later tried to tell her how good
it had been just to explain how he had felt about it all. 'It
really helps your heart feel better,' he said. 'Otherwise you
can worry all night!' Returning from school the next day
he told his mother how much easier it had been. Nothing
had really changed except that he had been able to share
his feelings with someone who had listened to him.

A young girl came to see us one day with the sad story
of a wrong relationship. This had resulted in heartbreak and
tragedy for her and her family. There was little we could
say, but occasionally one of us made a comment which we
hoped would indicate that we were listening and trying to
enter her world. After talking, crying and praying, she got
up to leave. Nothing had been resolved, nor in fact could
be, but she looked more peaceful. 'I feel much more settled
inside,' she said. 'It was such a help to tell my story and
to feel I had been understood.'

'Some theorists have looked upon good communication
in the family as the ground of mental health and bad
communication as the mark of dysfunctionality.'[6] Where
there is a climate for good communication emotions are
brought out into the open instead of being buried. Those
who cannot talk about their feelings will usually find
themselves acting them out in some bizarre way.

It has been well said that 'the family that feels together
heals together'.

It adds to life

St John wrote to the 'chosen lady and her children'. He said that instead of writing he would much rather visit her and talk to her face to face, 'so that our joy may be complete' (2 John 12). Communication adds to our enjoyment of life. It enlarges our vision and brings us out of the captivity of our private, isolated world where the disease of introspection can so easily plague us. My own childhood, spent in the country, was mostly a very lonely one. I would read my Enid Blyton books and envy the 'Five' who had so many splendid adventures together. When I was ten a boy of my age came to live up the lane. He too was lonely and gradually we came out of our isolation and made friends. I felt myself becoming more alive in the next two years. My activities did not change very much. I still spent hours up trees or in the stables with my horse but just to have another person to share with added a whole new dimension to life.

It protects from evil

Satan is an undercover agent and loves the darkness. When we hide our feelings, our failures, our sins from one another it gives him an opportunity to confuse us and condemn us. 'This determination to "go it alone" also makes both Christians and non-Christians very vulnerable to Satan in the deepest recesses of our being . . . Problems such as anger, bitterness, unforgiveness, worry, fear and lust are to be kept out of sight, even though they fester within us and make us sick. Satan is then free to gnaw away at our emotional problems like a rat working under cover of darkness.'[7]

During a celebration in church one Sunday I saw a person I knew looking very downcast. I went to pray with her and after a while she began to share what a terrible failure she had been. She began to cry over her many mistakes and condemn herself. I did not try to argue with her about her sense of worthlessness, because that is the truth about all of us. Instead I pointed to the cross hanging on the wall in front of us and suggested she start receiving God's mercy. For a moment she struggled, part of her wanting to hold on to the condemnation she felt she deserved, and the other part desperately wanting to receive God's grace. Eventually she turned her face upward and lifted her hands to receive the mercy which was freely available to her. True communication had won through. She had brought her feelings out into the open where Satan could no longer gnaw away at them. She had come to a position where she was able to receive the truth.

In true communication we share ourselves with another person. It is the most precious gift we can offer to anyone. It is costly, it is risky, but it is infinitely worth making the effort.

Encouraging true communication

For the past three years our local pool has been opening for early-morning swimmers. At first only a few people took advantage of the early hour and we enjoyed plenty of space to go up and down in whatever way we wished. Recently, however, it became uncomfortably like Piccadilly Circus. We were bumped by the back-strokers, slowed down by the more leisurely ladies and nearly drowned by large men. We were fast becoming frustrated with our morning exercise. Then one day we arrived to find notices up over the pool. One displayed the words: 'Slow Lane'. Another: 'Medium Lane', and yet another: 'Fast Lane'. Each notice had arrows pointing in a clockwise direction. So we sorted ourselves out into our lanes and began to swim according to the new directions. It worked! So long as everyone keeps to the rules the pleasure is back.

Good communication demands obedience to certain rules. If we keep to them we shall reap the benefits. If not we may get hurt and decide, as I heard a girl say recently, 'I am just no good at relationships.' We may not be good as yet but 'practice makes perfect'.

Choose the right person

We shall always need to be wise about how, when and with whom we share. An immature, inexperienced person may be unable to cope with another's hard or difficult feelings. A judgmental and critical person may be unable to resist interrupting with an 'ought' or a 'should'.

Dr Tournier, writing about the problem of finding good support in our human weakness, describes the right type of person with whom we can safely share ourselves:

> What we are looking for is not someone who will cut through our dilemmas for us, but someone who will try to understand them. Not someone who will impose his will upon us, but someone who will help us to use our own will. Someone who, instead of dictating to us what we must do, will listen to us with respect. Not someone who will reduce everything to an academic argument, but someone who will understand our personal motives, our feelings and even our weakness and our mistakes. Someone who will give us confidence in ourselves because he has unshakable confidence in us, who will take an interest in our struggles without pre-judging their outcome, who will not allow himself to be discouraged if we take a different road from the one he would have taken.[8]

We shall need to choose someone who will not only listen but who is prepared to share at the same depth. In a counselling relationship the counsellor should not be too ready to share his feelings with the counsellee because it is more important that he be a good listener, but at least he should be prepared to disclose his feelings should it seem appropriate.

Choose the right moment

When we have found the right person we must take it slowly and share a little at a time. We must also be sure that it is the best moment for such sharing. The right time is important when sharing feelings, both for the listener and the teller. It is always a good idea to ask if the other person has the time to spare before one gets launched. The receiver must take the risk of saying if it is not a good moment for in-depth sharing but at the same time convey the message that he wants to hear and would like to fix another time to meet. In our house it would be folly to start sharing something of importance just as the six o'clock news is about to come on. Bath-time, however, is relaxed and unpressured and seems to be the best time for us to communicate our ideas and our feelings with each other.

Make a start and stick at it

Having chosen the right person and settled for an appropriate time, risk and share more of yourself than previously. Practice makes perfect in any activity. Therefore having made a start resist the temptation to back away with a sigh of relief, thinking that because you have taken a risk you can now rest on your laurels. As you repeat the activity it will become easier.

Sometimes a person who has had a problem sharing intimately with others at the first attempt may find himself almost overwhelmed with difficult feelings, such as shame and guilt. 'I should never have said that.' Or, 'Now they will despise me,' are some of the thoughts which come into the mind. A counsellee recently told me that she had shared a problem with a new friend and was immediately filled with fear and regret. She believed she had made a terrible mistake. It was then a complete surprise and a great relief when the friend made a special effort to see her again and made it plain that she enjoyed her company.

Having chosen the right person and made a start we need to be wise in the way we communicate.

Avoid the pitfalls

Communication is a valuable tool in the growth process but can easily become a destructive implement when used improperly. Manipulation, blaming, punishing and making demands are all feelingful ways of conversing but the motivation is selfish and not based on a real desire for growth.

However, even honest communication can become manipulative and demanding, when done thoughtlessly. One of the ways of avoiding these pitfalls is first to examine one's motives and then to sift out any possible selfish element involved; then one is ready to share one's feelings. However, give the listener directions on how to receive what is about to be shared. For example, if one decides to share a recent feeling of rejection with one's friend, first look at the motives for sharing. Ask such questions as: 'Do I want to punish, blame, manipulate or dump my rubbish on her?' Find a way of sharing feelings of rejection which are devoid of such counter-productive motives. If one says, 'I felt rejected the other day when you spent so long with Anne,' the listener could feel guilty, responsible, manipulated into changing his/her behaviour or even to becoming secretive. It would be better to say, 'I would like to share some difficult feelings with you, which I know are immature and irrational. I don't want you to feel guilty or in any way to change your behaviour in order to protect me from my bad feelings. My motive is to share them so that you can help me to face them and perhaps discover why they are so painful.' In this way he/she will be reassured that this is an honest communication and the reason for sharing is a real desire for growth.

Another pitfall to avoid is that of subtly making demands upon the other person. We make a demand when we share a difficult feeling and then let the other person know that we expect them to resolve it for us. This way communication soon becomes a burden not a gift. We must take responsibility for our feelings and for finding ways through the bad ones, not expecting others to find the answers, only to favour us with understanding and support.

Commit to communicate

Last of all we can encourage communication by committing ourselves to it. As John Powell says, 'it has to be a flint-hard posture of the will, an inner resolution, a firm promise made to ourselves and to others with whom we are trying to relate.'

> I am determined to work at this, to give it all I've got. This commitment is unconditional: no fine print in the contract, no 'ifs' or 'buts' or time limits. I will work at it when it is easy and when it is difficult. I will try to tell you who I am. And I will listen to learn who you are. I will do this when I feel like it and even when I don't feel like it. I promise to hang in there with you even when the child in me would rather play games, pout, or punish you. I promise to hang in there even when I feel like quitting. Together we will work at sharing until we have built strong lines of communication. Only then can we experience the personal fulfilment that comes with effective communication.[9]

First there has to be a commitment to communicate. The

next concern is 'what' one communicates. Careless and insincere sharing will not enhance one's growth. Therefore dedication to the following discipline will be important.

Exercises

1. On which level do you feel most comfortable communicating? Experiment with your group/friend using each level of communication. Stop at the one that makes you feel uncomfortable.

2. Is there anyone in your life with whom you have peak-level communication?

3. Share with your group/friend/journal a time when someone communicated very meaningfully to you without words. How did it make you feel?

4. Is there anything in your personal history which could prevent you enjoying good communication with others?

5. Share with your group/friend/journal a difficult feeling you have recently experienced such as anger, jealousy, sadness, loneliness and at the same time take pains to avoid the pitfalls of blaming, punishing or making demands.

6. Spend time praying for any member of the group who would like to know the reason behind a difficult feeling, experienced seemingly without cause. Ask the Holy Spirit to come and uncover the truth. Give God time to do this.

7. If it is appropriate (and you feel it would help you) read the commitment on page 100 aloud to the group. Is there someone other than the group with whom you would like to make this commitment? What is stopping you?

8.   DEDICATION TO TRUTH

> ' "I will set out and go back to my father and say
> to him: Father, I have *sinned* against heaven and
> against you" ' (Luke 15:18).

The prodigal son reviewed his situation and faced up to the
painful truth that what he had done was 'sin'. This was not
simply some error of judgment, nor an unconscious mistake.
He had wilfully chosen to go his own way and do his own
thing. He had sinned against God for rejecting God's way
and sinned against his father for demanding his inheritance
prematurely and causing his father worry and heartache. The
prodigal did not avoid the truth. It must have been painful,
uncomfortable − even shameful − but he faced reality and
then went to his father and owned up.

The truth is frequently uncomfortable and humbling. To
be dedicated to truth is an essential, if difficult, discipline for
the Christian disciple. Yet many avoid it and do not realise
that by so doing they forgo a close relationship with Jesus who
said, 'I am the way and the truth and the life' (John 14:6).
Avoidance of truth is one of the deceptions we use to protect
the damaged inner-self from pain. It is part of the 'survival
kit' we have constructed over the years and used continuously
until it becomes a part of the very fabric of our personality.

Before we can begin to implement this discipline more
thoroughly, we must first recognise our economical use of
truth. Also we should understand the motivations behind
our prevarications.

Our economical use of truth

Truth has to be an important issue for every Christian, yet it is not easy to live a life of total truthfulness. We so easily tell, live and believe lies.

Speaking lies

Sometimes we employ *half-truths* in order not to cause offence or hurt, but often our motives for telling half-truths are more for reasons of *self-protection* than fear of offending others. It is easier to say what we think other people want to hear than be unpopular. But if we fail to side with the truth all parties become the losers.

When my husband was still a curate in Oxford he had a landlady who would always ask his opinion if she bought anything new. Whenever they have met since she reminds him of this. 'You were the only one whom I could trust to tell me the truth.' However painful it was, she preferred the truth to the half-truths she might receive from others.

Exaggeration is a common habit and few people would call it lying. Most of us women would hardly think twice about using some exaggeration in our conversation. Yet it is as much a lie to say, 'I didn't sleep at all last night,' meaning one slept badly, as it is to say, 'I slept well,' when in fact one had had a lousy night. Exaggeration has become so acceptable that it is regarded as a coded message that everyone is expected to decipher. Just cut it in half and divide by two and there you have the truth!

Why do people use exaggeration so much in our society? Behind the lie could lurk the *fear of feeling worthless*. An uninteresting and boring person is not listened to. It is a devastating experience to have someone turn away in apparent disinterest when one is talking. It has the power to turn a grown person into a tongue-tied, awkward teenager. To avoid this discomfort one learns to describe situations in life in exaggerated terms to make a 'good' story.

Another reason for exaggeration is the *need for sympathy*. To say, 'I didn't sleep at all last night,' is calculated to evoke more sympathy than, 'I didn't sleep very well last night.' 'Well what about it? Neither did I,' is the kind of brush-off response most feared. It would be nearer the truth to say, 'I didn't sleep very well last night, and I feel in need of a bit of sympathy.' Most people would respond positively to such honesty.

An *outright lie* is the most obvious form of avoiding the truth. Sometimes we differentiate between black and white lies. We feel that a little white lie is acceptable because it harms no one. A black lie, however, would be harmful and therefore wrong. We have all indulged in both at some time or another. Probably we have felt guilty and at least confessed the latter to God, but the former causes only momentary discomfort, if that. It is soon forgotten and laid to rest with the other hundred or so!

In our western world today the lies told by Ananias and Sapphira would be considered white ones (Acts 5). Surely they harmed no one? They could be viewed simply as suppressing part of the truth or even as exaggerations. The fact was it was deception. Ananias and Sapphira wanted to *impress others* by appearing more generous, more spiritual, more sacrificial than they actually were — a familiar motive we all understand. Although by today's standards it may be considered 'only a white lie', they had failed the honesty test in God's eyes; they had engaged in serious deception. The Father of Lies had snared them. We too readily forget how offensive our lies are to God. 'God is light; in him there is no darkness at all. If we claim to have fellowship with him yet walk in the darkness, we lie and do not live by the truth' (1 John 1:5,6).

I learned this a number of years ago in a very embarrassing and humiliating manner. It was a Tuesday morning, our day

off, and we had stayed in bed rather late. The door bell
sounded. I quickly pulled on some clothes and rushed
downstairs to answer it. On the doorstep stood an elderly
man who I knew only slightly. He must have spotted my
rather dishevelled state and said that he hoped he had not
got me out of bed. Without thinking, I assured him that
he had not. As soon as the words were out of my mouth
I regretted the lie but I rationalised that I had only tried to
protect him from feeling embarrassed at disturbing us. I said
a quick sorry to God and forgot the incident.

About a year later I was attending an early-morning
prayer meeting when, out of the blue, the memory of that
little white lie flashed into my mind. I hastily pushed it to
one side, but the memory persisted. I felt acutely
uncomfortable and wondered why God had reminded me
of it. I tried saying sorry again, but that did not resolve it.
Eventually I asked God if He was asking me to confess the
sin to the man in question. With a sinking heart I began
to sense that He was. In the end I decided to strike a
ridiculous bargain with God. I told Him I would be willing
to confess the sin to the man if God would arrange for him
to come to my house by 11 a.m. that morning. Should he
not arrive by that time I felt I could then forget the whole
thing and trust that there was nothing more I should do
about it. I was pretty confident of this arrangement with
God. It was well balanced in my favour. I had not seen the
said gentleman to talk to since that morning the previous
year and he certainly had not called at the house during that
time.

Just after ten that morning the door bell rang. On the
doorstep stood the very man. I thought I would faint with
fright! He had come to see my husband David about
something, so I showed him into the house and put on the
kettle to make him a cup of coffee. While David talked to
him I nipped upstairs to pray an urgent prayer. 'Oh God,
Oh God,' I pleaded, 'I don't think I can do what you are

asking of me. Certainly I can't do it with David present. If you really want me to do it then you will have to remove David for a few minutes.' I went downstairs and as I entered the kitchen David got up and told me he had to rush across to the church office for a short while. 'Darling, give Mr . . . some coffee, I'll be back soon.' With that he left us alone. My heart was in my mouth. For a moment my fear of looking a fool nearly overcame my fear of disobeying God. I took a deep breath and the confession came tumbling out. I don't think the poor man understood quite why I had been so concerned! He mumbled something which my embarrassment prevented me from hearing, and then David returned. My daily prayer since has been that God would keep my mouth from lies − black or white. I never want to be put through such an ordeal again.

In our conversation with others it is also possible to show a lack of dedication to the truth by *the manipulation of information for one's own ends*. This is done when we are selective with the truth in order to give a certain impression to our hearers which benefits us in some way. We justify ourselves that we have not lied. What we have shared has been correct; we have only omitted parts which did not fit with the story we wanted our hearers to believe. Nevertheless a lie has been perpetrated. The driving force behind this sort of activity is usually fear. *Fear of losing one's reputation or one's position*. Often there is a need to bolster up a low *self-image*. Misinformation of this sort can quickly gather momentum in a church fellowship, setting brother against brother. It is an activity in which Satan delights.

Living a lie

We fail to embrace truth when we use *masks, pretences and subterfuges*. Although risky, truth demands we are transparent with other people.

Being acceptable to others adds to our sense of well being

and self-worth. Being unacceptable involves a sense of devaluation which is very painful. To avoid this pain we quickly learn to hide the apparently unacceptable bit of ourselves and exhibit to the world only those parts we think will be acceptable or liked. Unfortunately, at times of pressure and crisis the less acceptable parts of the self have a tendency to surface. A young woman sat in my study recently and cried in despair. 'I'm coming apart. Soon everyone will know what I'm really like.' Everyone knew her as a very competent and efficient nurse. This was all true but it was only a part of the truth. Few knew about the anxious, vulnerable part of her; this was her secret-self who in her mind was quite unacceptable and must never be seen. This part caused her to live a lie and even occasionally to tell a lie. She felt she had to protect this hidden-self at all cost.

Vulnerability, anxiety, panic attacks and loneliness; these sorts of feeling are regarded as weak and shameful by some. They will go to great lengths to hide such feelings and the fear of their discovery only adds to the anxiety. Many choose to cover their perceived weakness with drugs or alcohol, often pretending to themselves and to others that they have no chemical or alcohol dependency. An extremely shy man I know is a secret drinker. He has fooled his family for years into thinking he is teetotal. Another young woman suffers from severe panic attacks and anxiety which are reasonably controlled with medication. No one even suspects her problem because she covers it so well with laughter and jokes. Occasionally, however, she is forced to leave the room in a hurry to prevent anyone from seeing her hands shaking.

Being transparent also means taking care that one's private life corresponds with one's public life. *Hypocrisy* is a form of lying which was abhorrent to Jesus:

"Woe to you, teachers of the law and Pharisees, you hypocrites! You clean the outside of the cup and dish, but inside they are full of greed and self-indulgence. Blind Pharisee! First clean the inside of the cup and dish, and then the outside also will be clean.

"Woe to you, teachers of the law and Pharisees, you hypocrites! You are like whitewashed tombs, which look beautiful on the outside but on the inside are full of dead men's bones and everything unclean. In the same way, on the outside you appear to people as righteous but on the inside you are full of hypocrisy and wickedness" (Matt.23:25–8).

Hypocrisy is a lie of proud pretence. It is an outward show to deceive others. It says one thing and thinks another. It lives one way in public and another in private. The hypocrite believes his own lie. He believes that what cannot be seen or known does not really matter or even exist. He is so concerned with a good self-projection that he has no time for self-examination. He is like the man who went up to the temple and thanked God for not making him like other men – robbers, evildoers, adulterers. He was a Pharisee, a church leader of his day, but he failed to go home justified. The tax collector, however, who beat his breast and said to God, 'Have mercy on me, a sinner,' did go home justified. One had looked at God and then his own heart and realised the truth. The other had failed to recognise God and glowed with his own self-righteousness. (Luke 18:9–14).

Recently the Christian world has been shocked and saddened by scandals concerning certain US televangelists. These men have lived in public as if they were righteous, God-fearing men. Privately they were being seriously disobedient to Him. Their hypocrisy has become common knowledge. Yet how many ordinary Christian men and women live with similar duplicity?

Hypocrisy belongs to both the sexes. It is an easy sin to fall into and a hard one to fight against because of the dividends it seems to pay. I remember once agreeing to do a book-signing session. I sat at a table while people queued for me to sign a book I had written. By the time I had been there an hour I began to feel quite important. It was tempting to believe it! None of those nice people knew the real me. They didn't know my failures or my sins. They hadn't seen me fed-up and bad tempered. All they saw was someone trying to look dignified in her best outfit! How easy for me to fall into the trap of hypocrisy, since it is ego boosting to be well thought of by others who have no real opportunity for knowing the truth. Then, as other people swallow the lie we are projecting, our pride grows and it becomes increasingly difficult to lay aside the mask and be real. One may even start to believe the lie and consider oneself special, or important, or better than others. This kind of self-worth depends upon pretence.

The way we manage to live with hypocrisy is by *rationalisation and denial*. 'I'm not doing anyone else harm;' 'It's just an occasional indulgence;' 'Everyone loses their tempers now and again;' or, 'Children have short memories.' I once heard a Christian father rationalising his incest on the grounds that he believed the victim had liked it!

When we live in denial we *avoid the painful truth about our hurting inner-self;* we also *avoid the uncomfortable truth about our sinful reactions*. We seek to create the illusion of peace and happiness which, although false, is preferable to the unhappy, painful reality. One way this may be done is by creating a fantasy childhood which never really existed. Barbara Gordon, mentioned earlier, was helped to face her past and come out of denial. Her therapist said to her, 'It's good for you to talk about it. For the first time in your life you are looking at yourself. You alone, without pills, looking at your life. It's important to know it all.'[1] Reflecting on her experience towards the end of the book, she recollects one of the inmates saying that neurosis is lying. 'Give up lies and you're there.' To this she adds, 'All the subconscious lies, the well meaning lies, that protect us from the truth about loving and unloving, we sometimes think we need for survival. But they are the seeds of destruction of love and reality and truth.'[2] Coming to terms with the reality of her childhood was an important part of the healing process for Barbara.

We use denial as a *protection from the pain of past memories*. We use it to prevent ourselves from accepting that our parents were not always good. Our eldest daughter recently shared that it was a bad experience for her to be sent back from home in South America to attend a boarding school in England. Having listened to her, I expressed my regret at having made the decision to send her back. She began hastily to deny our responsibility. 'No, no. It wasn't your fault. You had to make that choice.' I pointed out to her that we could have made a different one, but we didn't. We were responsible for making a choice that caused her to suffer. We were to blame and she had to face that truth. How else could she forgive us? Before we can release forgiveness to those who have hurt us we first have to face the painful truth of their failure or sin.

We also have a tendency to rationalise away our sins by calling them mistakes, or blunders. Rarely do we admit what the prodigal son said, 'I have sinned.' In March, 1970, we were on a ship, crossing from England to South America. I had come to a place of desperation in my life and longed for God to renew me. I spent most evenings secluded in a quiet corner of the deck praying. I kept asking God to fill me with His Spirit but nothing appeared to happen. I wondered whether something was blocking me from receiving. I began to examine my life. 'Oh, Lord,' I prayed, 'if I sinned when I did "such and such", or if I sinned when I said "thus and so", please forgive me.' Nothing! The heavens seemed like brass. I tried again. 'Lord, if I sinned when . . .' Then I realised what I was saying. By using that little word 'if' I was trying to evade responsibility for my sin. I was not fully admitting that what I had done, or said, was sin. So I changed my prayer to, 'Lord, I sinned when I said such and such, or when I did thus and so. Please forgive me.' Little by little I went through my life owning and repenting for my sins. I found it very hard and to my knowledge it was the first time I had ever confessed my sin without using that little word 'if'. It was soon after this that God graciously met me in a most remarkable and unforgettable way, and renewed my whole life.

In counselling there will be no healing or change until a counsellee comes out of denial and faces the truth about himself, about his past, about his life and about his sin. Sin must be called by its rightful name. Until there is a heartfelt repentance, which is quite distinct from sorrow or remorse, our besetting sins will continue to have power over us.

Suppression is another common method employed for *avoiding painful feelings*. It gives the impression of strength and togetherness rather than of weakness and vulnerability. It is a way of lying both to ourselves and to others. Like King David, all of us must come to terms with the fact that the Lord desires truth in the inner parts (Ps.51:6).

Most of us have grown up in a world where suppression is considered normal and respectable. To express emotion would be immature and embarrassing. Many people learn to suppress or at least mask their feelings from an early age. They learn it formally and informally; through teaching and through example. Unfortunately those feelings do not die when suppressed; they simply live on but now in a masked form. I have heard it said, 'That which we do not speak out we will act out.' This 'acting out' of suppressed feelings is usually unhealthy and destructive – a sinful response to inner pain. John Powell says that by repressing our emotions we are hiding the source of our pain in the 'dungeon' of the subconscious. 'Repressed emotions unfortunately do not die. They refuse to be silenced. They pervasively influence the whole personality and behaviour of the repressor.'[3] He goes on to say that 'buried emotions are like rejected people; they make us pay a high price for having rejected them. Hell hath no fury like that of a scorned emotion.'[4]

We have all met those who have found it very difficult to express grief over the passing of a loved one. They have tried to be brave and not to embarrass anyone with their tears. Then, within months of their bereavement, they have become ill. One such person developed a stomach ulcer within a year of his wife's death. The unexpressed grief was gnawing his very guts.

Sometimes the feelings seem so 'unacceptable' that we try to strangle them at birth. By stifling them in this way we not only miss out on what they could tell us, but we could end up by 'acting them out' in some slightly bizarre manner.

A young girl told me that she had recently suffered acute pain when her close friend spent a lot of time with someone else. Jealousy and possessiveness were the labels she gave to the feelings. These were so 'unacceptable' that she immediately buried them. The next day, however, she woke feeling depressed and ill. Her depression caused her to ask for prayer. As the suppressed feelings surfaced during the prayer time, so too did the truth. The mislabelled emotions were properly identified as fear of loss. This fear had been caused in the first place by a traumatic childhood separation and had been re-stimulated by her friend's behaviour. Once the truth was faced the depression began to lift.

As we have seen, repression can lead to ill health, poor relationships and, more seriously, to stunted growth. '. . . the essential tragedy of repression is that the whole process of human growth is shut down, at least temporarily.'[5]

Believing lies

Devotion to the truth will involve us in the ongoing process of having our minds renewed. Healthy Christian development is blocked when a person continues to hold irrational beliefs concerning themselves, others and life in general. Growth is stunted especially when we retain misconceptions about God. We may hold on to these beliefs to suit ourselves.

God miraculously rescued the Jews from slavery in Egypt. He proved His love and care for them over and over again and yet they chose to remain rebellious and unconvinced. Despite amazing manifestations of God's love for them and of His power to save them the Israelites were too frightened to enter the promised land. They excused their cowardice by resorting to a misinterpretation of God. They grumbled in their tents saying, 'The Lord hates us; so he brought us out of Egypt to deliver us into the hands of the Amorites to destroy us' (Deut.1:26,27). By persuading themselves that God was as depraved and destructive as their old masters, the Pharaohs of Egypt, they were unprepared to take on the Amorites in battle. Their misrepresentation of God made Him into a cruel monster.

It suits us sometimes to believe God to be benevolent and kindly. Surely He is a God who winks at our sinful indulgences and forgives us as we confess the same faults over again, even though we are making no effort to change. Richard Lovelace observes a sentimentalising of God coming out of the late nineteenth century. 'The whole Church was drifting quietly . . . avoiding the Biblical portrait of the sovereign and holy God who is angry with the wicked every day and whose anger remains upon those who will not receive his Son . . . The Church substituted a new god who was the projection of grandmotherly kindness mixed with the gentleness and winsomeness of a Jesus who hardly needed to die for our sins.'[6]

As we draw near to Lent people think of things they might give up for those few weeks. One young couple told their pastor that they had decided to give up sleeping together for Lent. The fact that they were not married and should not be sleeping together anyway did not seem to bother them. Spiritual darkness becomes complete when we abandon the worship of the true God for a magnified image of human tolerance. By making Him in our own image we cease to have a healthy fear of a Holy God.

Of course there will always be a tension between God's mercy and His holy righteousness. But, as Lovelace goes on to say, 'There is only one way that this contradiction can be removed: through the cross of Christ which reveals the severity of God's anger against sin and the depth of His compassion in paying its penalty through the vicarious sacrifice of his Son.'[7]

So it is possible to misrepresent God to suit ourselves. We may also do it to fit our distorted view of authority. The Israelites perceived God as they had perceived their past Egyptian masters. All of us have a tendency to transfer our reactions from the past into the present. Our view of authority may be distorted by a bad past experience. We then bring this distortion into the present and perceive every authority figure, including God, in the same way.

Such irrational ways of perceiving God can greatly impede our growth as Christians. Today's society suffers from 'the absentee father' syndrome. Either it is a one-parent family for reasons of divorce, death or illegitimacy, or it is the workaholic father, seen only at weekends, and too exhausted to do more than fall asleep behind his Sunday newspaper. We are ministering to more and more people who are transferring their limited and personal experience of a father onto God Himself. He is viewed as distant, absent, disinterested or unreal. Consequently their reaction is often angry and resentful. Because of His perceived disinterest and lack of care, He is blamed for all their troubles.

The misrepresentation could also be due to past teaching. Some people have been taught that God is a stern judge who punishes every misdemeanour. Such one-sidedness shuts down all spontaneity and freedom. Children brought up under such teaching will usually turn out in one of two ways.

Either totally rebellious and wanting nothing to do with such a God, or absolute perfectionists, serving God fearfully, but with little enjoyment. They will need a radical change in their concept of God and it takes a disciplined effort to be 'made new in the attitude' of our minds (Eph.4:23). It is often easier to remain with our old assumptions about God. Distortions such as these will keep us as immature, resentful children for the rest of our lives.

Encouraging dedication to truth

This discipline is vital for our mental, emotional and spiritual health. Therefore we must encourage its consistent use.

By daring to pray

God will show us our hearts when we pray as the psalmist prayed: 'Search me, O God, and know my heart; test me and know my anxious thoughts. See if there is any offensive way in me, and lead me in the way everlasting' (Ps.139:23,24). The way everlasting is the way of truth. Only when we see ourselves for what we really are can we truly repent and be forgiven. It is only the cleansed, forgiven sinner who finds himself on 'the way everlasting'. The hypocrite continues proudly and blindly on the path towards judgment.

As we pray for God to search our hearts we must let Him walk back through the secret corridors of our lives, searching every nook and cranny. Our lives must become an open book to Him. It is of course impossible not to sin and at times we will practise the various forms of lying mentioned above, but such things are always more easily put right immediately than later. If we can develop an open ear for the still small voice of God and react to it sooner rather than later, we will quickly find ourselves enjoying intimacy with

God along with closeness to our brothers and sisters in Christ.

By daring to look first at God and then at ourselves

Today, as I write this, many Christians worldwide are praying for revival. When this happens, eyes will be opened to see God and people will see themselves as God sees them. 'What men wake up to in the light of a revival is their own condition and the nature of the true God.'[8] When God shows us His holiness even our good deeds seem like rags and tatters.

On receiving visions of God both Isaiah and Job became acutely aware of their own sin. 'Woe to me!' Isaiah cried. 'I am ruined! For I am a man of unclean lips, and I live among a people of unclean lips, and my eyes have seen the King, the Lord Almighty' (Is.6:5). 'My ears had heard of you,' said Job, 'but now my eyes have seen you. Therefore I despise myself and repent in dust and ashes' (Job 42:5,6).

There is great need for a fresh vision of God today; for us to catch a glimpse of the God of the Bible, not some image that we have concocted out of our imagination to suit ourselves, nor a God of some past experience or past teaching. Only as we search the Scriptures will we find the truth — first about God and then, in the light of that truth, about ourselves.

After one sermon a lady complained that she didn't like so much talk about revival. 'God is more merciful than to uncover our sin,' she said. 'But that is God's mercy,' I replied. 'It is God's mercy to show us our sin so that we can confess and repent of it. Only then can we receive His forgiveness. Until that moment we go blindly on meriting only His judgment.' One of the ways we become aware of our sin is when we catch a glimpse of the purity of God. Then we fall on our faces in repentance and worship.

By daring to be confronted and challenged by others

Only when we love one another do we trust one another enough to be open and vulnerable. A tiniest challenge from a friend concerning behaviour or conversation will tend to be perceived as criticism by those suffering from a low self-image. The Father of Lies has most of us tied up in knots over criticism. We have fed on the lie that criticism decreases our value. The fact is that our true value has been fixed once and for all. There is no such thing as deflation or inflation with regard to our soul's worth before God. When He chose to die for us He put a price upon us way beyond the price of silver, gold or precious stones. Nothing can minimise that value. Yet Satan persists in tempting us to believe that our real worth is dependent upon the approval of others — and we fall for it nearly every time!

Opening our lives to confrontation and challenge from friends, as well as from God, shows dedication to truth. Occasionally we have been called upon to counsel families having problems. I am always humbled when a Christian couple in the church asks if they may come as a family and talk about their difficulties. By doing this they virtually undress in our presence. One such family had hit a bad patch with their teenage daughter. She was angry and resentful towards her mother and younger sister. Not being able to find a way through by themselves they eventually asked for help.

It was extremely painful for both the parents to be confronted and challenged by their two children. In the first session I remember the younger one spelling out quite clearly how she perceived the family as each living in their own space, never touching one another. More truth began to emerge as the sessions continued and on one particularly painful occasion the eldest daughter described her feelings at the time of her younger sister's birth. It explained so much about her subsequent behaviour. The parents bravely heard

their children through and on more than one occasion wept
with them. Gradually all the painful feelings were out in the
open and one could sense the healing beginning. My
colleague and I watched an amazing transformation taking
place and it was largely due to the whole family's courage
in facing the difficult issues fairly and squarely. They were
prepared for confrontation with the truth.

Dedication to truth is a must if growth and maturity are
to occur. Very little headway can be made in a counselling
relationship when a counsellee imparts an unspoken threat
to his counsellor. The message is that confrontation with
the truth will be dangerous: 'If you do, I might get worse,
or commit suicide, or run away, or never trust you again.'
When truth is avoided in this way, so also is discomfort,
but sadly the opportunity for growth may be lost too.

'It is important for our growth to take all the
opportunities that present themselves, to learn how to accept
criticism and to handle times of dryness and failure, with
honesty,' writes Grace Sheppard. 'Not to acknowledge these
feelings of dryness or failure can lead to self-deception and
prevent us from growing healthily. Opening ourselves up
to face these times is a risk worth taking. We discover more
about ourselves, and more about the love and acceptance
of God. This helps us to feel less alone and more alive.'[9]

By allowing our discomfort to challenge us

In our dedication to truth it is important to become aware
of the messages our emotions and our bodies may be
sending. Frequently dis-ease within alerts us to something
wrong in our lives. Certainly some form of discomfort will
follow suppression of feelings. John Powell encourages us
to use discomfort as a teacher and not run away from it.
Instead he suggests that we should examine it because our
discomfort may be a signal ready to offer us an important
lesson.[10] Dedication to truth will therefore involve self-

examination. It will mean taking the time to allow any disease to speak and tell its message.

Not long ago I accidently overheard some criticism of myself. Someone observed that I had not been very friendly to herself and others. I did not react to the criticism in any way except to note it. The following Sunday I arrived at church fairly early to make sure I was there to greet people as they came through the door. Suddenly a lady came up to distract me from my self-imposed task. She was in some distress and wanting to talk — not an unusual happening and one I usually take in my stride. However on this occasion I began to feel nausea as she poured out her story. On top of the nausea I began to feel tearful and wanted to run away. I was completely baffled by such a bizarre reaction. Eventually I was able to free myself from the lady and go and sit down. I closed my eyes and let my extreme discomfort speak to me. Immediately the words of criticism came back to me. I realised that unconsciously I had been trying to counter it by being extra-friendly to everyone. Then the troubled lady had prevented me from greeting the people coming in through the church door. The more time she took up talking, the more people I was unable to greet. I had begun to feel sick and tearful with the realisation that however much I tried I could never be what other people wanted me to be. In those moments of quiet my discomfort had become my teacher.

The benefits of dedication to the truth

Besides the important objective of growing and becoming more like Jesus, devotion to the truth brings other benefits to one's life.

Forgiveness

'If we confess our sins, he is faithful and just and will forgive us our sins and purify us from all unrighteousness' (1 John 1:9). God can heal or forgive what is brought into the light. Satan has the power to use what is kept in the darkness against us. When a counsellee is having a job telling me something he or she considers shameful I always encourage them to make the effort to disclose it. 'It's much better out than in. God can deal with it once it's in the open.' Hidden and unconfessed sins can make us sick. That sickness may start within our hearts but will often permeate our whole beings and in a while we are also manifesting sickness in our bodies. James encourages us to confess our sins to one another so that we may be healed (James 5:16).

A few years ago a young man came to see me to ask if he should tell his wife that before becoming a Christian he had once been unfaithful to her. This matter had been on his conscience ever since his conversion and he wanted there to be truth between the two of them. I could appreciate his motive for bringing this matter out in the open but was unsure that he should burden her with a sin that had been forgiven and forgotten by God. At the same time I was aware that the one-flesh union had been broken and that this might be affecting his wife in some way. After we prayed together I suggested he keep himself open to telling his wife, and trust that God would make it clear to him if ever or whenever it would be appropriate to do so. It was more than a year later that the opportunity occurred and he was able to confess it to his wife. When he heard her words of forgiveness he finally felt forgiven. It had come about quite naturally in this case and had resulted in greater intimacy and oneness. On the other hand I have heard of a very similar confession being made which resulted in the wife divorcing the husband for infidelity. These delicate situations need handling with a great deal of love and sensitivity.

'It is true that, in all communication, kindness without honesty is sentimentality; but it is likewise true that honesty without kindness is cruelty.'[11]

Freedom

Jesus said 'Then you will know the truth, and the truth will set you free' (John 8:32). Hiding, lying, covering up, all take effort. One lie often leads to another, and then another. The perpetrator of a lie lives in fear of it being discovered. He has to remember what impression he gave last time he saw you, or how he explained a certain experience. Usually it is too hard to keep up and eventually the lie is found out.

A young girl lied continually to her counsellor. One day her counsellor, bewildered by the confusing messages she was receiving, challenged the young girl about being economical with the truth. The girl confessed that she was afraid her counsellor would refuse to see her if she told the real truth. When they met again for the next counselling session she explained that she had thought about telling her usual lies but had decided against it since: 'I knew I would probably contradict myself and you would find me out. I decided it was too much hassle to lie.'

An increasing sense of lightness and freedom comes as we seek out and believe the truth about God and His attitude towards us. Once a person who has believed all his life that he should never have been born and has no right to be alive finally accepts the truth that he was foreknown and predestined (Rom.8:29) and that he is chosen and dearly loved by God (Col.3:12), his whole concept of himself changes. He comes out of prison and into the glorious freedom of the sons of God.

Fellowship

'But if we walk in the light, as he is in the light, we have fellowship with one another, and the blood of Jesus, his Son purifies us from all sin,' (1 John 1:7). The truth brings us into fellowship with the One who said He was the Truth. When we avoid the truth in any way we forfeit that fellowship. It also brings us into fellowship with one another. Masks, pretences, hypocrisy, half-truths, all place barriers between ourselves and others. There is no real community amongst believers where these things exist. Openness and truth bind us together in a common understanding.

Many of us long for greater intimacy in our walk with God and with one another. We will only gain this if we are prepared to face the discomfort of becoming more transparent and truthful. There are many benefits, not least of which is maturity and growth.

The prodigal took the first steps of his homeward journey when he faced up to the truth. However, before he could fully enjoy the healing presence of his father, he had to sever every link with the far country. Having reached such a point of desperation, his surrender was relatively easy. But easy or difficult, the journey towards wholeness involves us all in the next discipline of relinquishment and exchange.

Exercises

1. Are you aware of avoiding the truth by any of the means mentioned in this chapter? What is the driving force behind this habit?

2. Do you feel there are parts of yourself or your life you must hide from others? What is your motive for hiding the truth? If you can, share this with your group/friend.

3. Having read the chapter, are you aware of holding any distorted beliefs about God? What has caused this distortion? Share this with your group/friend/journal and together look for a Biblical corrective for the distortion. Write this down in your journal and pray it through with God daily until the truth takes root.

4. How do you feel about being confronted by a friend or conversely confronting a friend? Is your value at stake here?

5. Have you experienced recent discomfort, either emotional or physical, which you have ignored or suppressed? Take time now to listen to the message your dis-ease may be sending you.

6. Perhaps while reading the chapter or doing the exercises you have become aware of sin in your life. If this is the case you could confess it aloud to God and let one of the group pronounce God's forgiveness to you using the verse in 1 John 1, verse 9.

If the sin is too personal, confess it to God when on your own. It helps to say it aloud and to call it by its right name. Read 1 John 1, verse 9, and then stretch out your hands to receive the gift of God's forgiveness. Wait until you are sure that particular sin has now been dealt with.

7. End by passing the peace to one another as a gesture of love and acceptance.

9. RELINQUISHMENT AND EXCHANGE

' ". . . I am starving to death. I will . . . go back to my father' " . . . The father said to his servants, "Quick! Bring the best robe and put it on him. Put a ring on his finger and sandals on his feet. Bring the fattened calf and kill it. Let's have a feast and celebrate. For this son of mine was *dead* and is *alive again*; he was *lost* and is *found*" ' (Luke 15:17,22–4).

The prodigal son left the far country, exchanging it for his father's home and presence. He exchanged emptiness for fullness, pigs for family, death for life! Before coming to this position he must have struggled with all the implications of relinquishment. For a short while he had enjoyed the heady, addictive experience of total independence; of being in control of his own life. He had sampled all the glitter and excitement of the far country. However disastrous the experience had been, no one gives that up without a major struggle with pride.

Relinquishment and exchange take place throughout life. Many childhood tears have been shed over the 'letting go' of precious toys, familiar places, and habitual practices in order to 'take up' new, better or more appropriate ones. These experiences are frequently accompanied by painful feelings such as fear, insecurity and uncertainty. Often there may be considerable delay before the benefits of any exchange are experienced. Sometimes there appears to be no benefit in the exchange at all and we are left only with the pain of loss.

I remember as a child having to relinquish the warmth and safety of sharing my older sister's bed. The thought of exchanging my familiar place beside her for the privilege of my own space did not at first attract me. The 'letting go' was painful. The prospect was lonely. The benefits were only discovered gradually.

In 1959 the *Reina del Mar* 'PSSNC' pulled out of Liverpool docks heading for South America. The giving up of relatives, friends and homeland was accompanied by heartbreaking agony and fearful uncertainty. During the first years in Chile we could only view the exchange in terms of sacrifice. Much later, however, the great benefits became increasingly obvious to us. 'The Lord is no man's debtor.'

'Relinquishment and exchange' are inevitably part of the package of life. They only become disciplines when we deliberately choose to put them into practice for a particular purpose. They become Christian disciplines when we choose to practise them out of a will to obey God and a desire to become more Christ-like.

The struggle over their practice begins the moment we become Christians. Without being aware of all the issues, we begin the struggle to give up the old ways and embrace the new. The initial start is energetic and significant, but too often we stop short at change in the deeper aspects of our being. It takes a while to comprehend that God's desire for His children is total obedience and dependence upon Him. Just like Jesus. This is the kind of maturity God is seeking in us.

In our first chapter we looked at the fleshly 'survival kits' we have formed and used over the years. These devices keep the damaged inner-self from feeling too much pain or discomfort. They also serve to satisfy, if only momentarily, some of the unmet inner needs. The obviously sinful parts of this 'survival kit' are normally laid down when a person first becomes a Christian but too often the more subtle methods we employ to minimise our inner pain are retained, and continue as part of our pattern of life.

Christian maturity demands that we 'put off' our old self and 'put on' the new self created to be like God. For this to occur we will need the disciplines already mentioned. However, without finally 'letting go' the change will remain only hoped for and never fully accomplished.

A biblical perception

Throughout Scripture we find God urging His people to put this discipline into operation. Ever since the Fall, man has sought to find ways of meeting his own needs apart from God. As God says through Jeremiah: 'My people have committed two sins: They have forsaken me, the spring of living water, and have dug their own cisterns, broken cisterns that cannot hold water' (Jer.2:13). God constantly waits for men and women to leave their own ways and turn to Him for their strength, satisfaction and fulfilment. He says to them: 'How gladly would I treat you like sons . . . I thought you would call me "Father" and not turn away from following me' (Jer.3:19).

The Old Testament is full of characters who practised the discipline and were commended by God. Noah relinquished his reputation and built an ark in the face of criticism, thereby exchanging death for life. Abraham was commended because he left the security of his home and his country, exchanging them for the insecurity of the promised land. Moses gave up his privileged position in the palace of Pharaoh for identification with a collection of slaves. All these, and many more, sacrificed the familiar, safe paths for obedience and dependence on God. They were commended for their faith.

The New Testament is also full of challenges to give up

the old patterns of life and exchange them for new and godly ones. Paul instructed the Ephesian Christians to 'put off' the old defiled self and 'put on' the new purified self which has been created to be like God (Eph.4:22–4). In his letter to the Colossians he urges them to deal severely with the old carnal patterns. They must mortify those habitual ways of getting their needs met and put on the new self, which is being renewed in the knowledge and image of its Creator (Col.3:5,10).

Above all we have Jesus' famous words, which form the great challenge to Christians down the ages: 'If anyone would come after me, he must deny himself and take up his cross daily and follow me. For whoever wants to save his life will lose it, but whoever loses his life for me will save it. What good is it for a man to gain the whole world, and yet lose or forfeit his very self?' (Luke 9:23–5). In the days of Christ those who carried a cross were seen as on their way to death. They no longer had control of their own lives. That was in the hands of another. Jesus is here exhorting His followers to deny themselves the control of their own lives and to put themselves under God's control. It could be as painful and as difficult as dying.

Jesus also said, 'Anyone who loves his father or mother more than me is not worthy of me; anyone who loves his son or daughter more than me is not worthy of me' (Matt.10:37). A family usually provides security and a sense of belonging. Jesus confronts His disciples on the means they had hitherto employed for getting their security needs met. He challenges them to take the huge risk of giving up those habitual means. He encourages us all to depend upon Him and to experience the abundant life He offers us.

Relinquishing the 'survival kit'

God desires to meet all the inner needs of His children. He

longs to heal our brokenness, fill our emptiness and meet our loneliness. But while we spend time, effort and money exploring every other means for getting our needs met, He can only watch and wait. This was all the father could do for the prodigal son.

These self-devised methods we use to meet our needs, to minimise our pain and to give us good feelings are only temporarily successful. In the long term they serve to keep us from God's best. To achieve wholeness and maturity such practices will need to be discarded.

Before laying down a 'survival kit' one must be able to identify it in all its disguises. The sheer variety of devices we employ prevents us from making a comprehensive list of them. Nevertheless some are sufficiently common to be worth a mention.

The desire for security is a dominant drive within most people. Feelings of insecurity can create great emotional discomfort. One of the most common, although frequently unrecognised, methods by which we handle this is by making great efforts to control the details of our life.

Control

Everyone finds being out of control disturbing. We all have our daily rituals which give us a sense of security and continuity, not to mention the comfortable feeling that we have some power over our lives. However, there are certain people who take this need to control beyond normal limits. They only feel secure when they are compulsively attempting to control everything. They are often very disciplined people, organising and managing their lives and their environment with little rules and regulations. Such a person will always arrive five minutes early for an appointment in order to feel more secure. Inward comfort is achieved when everything is done by the book. Compulsive tidying and cleaning minimises his feeling of insecurity. The need to control is the dominant factor in his life. Many anorexics fall into this category. Where body shape and weight can be so drastically maintained by dieting the overwhelming fear of losing control is allayed — at least for a while.

A young girl I know had suffered a very deprived childhood. She sought to minimise her anxiety and insecurity by compulsive cleanliness. She concentrated considerable energies on becoming perfectly hygienic. In this way she felt she was controlling contamination with the bad around her, and gained a momentary peace by so doing. But as soon as another negative thought about her environment came to mind her fleeting feelings of security were scattered; her cleaning routine would begin all over again.

Control of others

There are those who control both their environment and others from their advantageous position of leadership. Delegation is far too threatening so they keep everything in their own hands. So long as they stay 'top dog' they can control those around them. These people only feel secure and of value when they are in charge.

Others feel they lose control when they are put in a position of receiving instead of giving. Receiving makes them feel insecure and vulnerable. They feel more 'in charge' when giving. A young woman I know had the embarrassing experience of being given a surprise party by her friends. They had gone to the trouble of making a special lunch with all her favourite food. They plied her with compliments and tried to convey to her their gratitude for all her kindness to them. As the lunch party progressed her discomfort increased. Eventually she thought up a way of regaining control and minimising her acute dis-ease. She persuaded them to come to her house the following week when she would cook a meal for them all — on her own! Only when she had paid her friends back with interest could she begin to regain control and thereby feel better. She was resorting to an habitual technique for escaping her bad feelings.

Control through negative self-talk

This is another way in which we minimise our insecurity. A person who finds it hard to commit himself to relationships may control his desire to do so with pessimistic thoughts. 'He will let me down if I come to depend upon him in any way.' Or, 'She will engulf me and become like clinging ivy. I must be careful!' Another person may control her fear of being unacceptable by telling herself to keep pleasing everyone. 'They will only like me if they need me.' Or, 'They will only accept me if I work hard.' A woman I know restricts her participation in a group by telling herself constantly that she is stupid. It precludes her from ever contributing in any significant way, but it also prevents her from re-experiencing the shame she suffered as a child.

These negative thoughts prevent behavioural changes and keep us locked into immature and unhealthy ways of being. They become so much a normal and habitual part of our lives that we are frequently unaware that we are even using them.

A special identity

Another compelling human need is to feel significant to other people and this is frequently met by making a name for oneself. The prodigal son was probably known in the far country by a name that gave him a distinctive identity: 'the gambler', or 'the dare-devil'. When he returned home he received back his true identity — his father's beloved son.

Each of us needs to be important to someone. We need the attention and love of others. So often we presume that these needs will only be met if we draw and hold other people's attention through adopting some compelling kind of identity. A 'victim' identity may be linked to a past happening, such as incest, abuse or rejection. Strangely a person with this sort of identity will often manipulate others into demonstrating it to be true. Thus, the 'rejected child' will make others reject her and by doing so prove that her adopted identity is true. The 'victim' believes himself to be continually victimised by others and gains sympathy by maintaining this identity. Others create an identity for themselves by behaving in certain ways. The 'nice-guy', the 'rescuer', the 'counsellor', the 'workaholic', the 'perfectionist', the 'sportsman', or the 'hypochondriac'. Each person lives out his chosen identity to lessen his fear of being a nobody. Until that is relinquished, he or she can never take up the new reality and become the 'beloved, chosen, child of God'.

Without a strong understanding of who we are in Christ we are denied that awareness of self-hood which is so vital for our sense of well-being.

Nearing the end of her illness, Barbara Gordon's new therapist told her quite bluntly that she needed to give up sickness as part of her personality. ' . . . in sickness you at least felt connected to something. Without love, without work, you lost your identity, and a sick identity became preferable to none.'[1]

A young man once told me that he had felt very unhappy because he knew everyone else enjoyed having their families around them. He was alone and had no immediate family. He explained rather proudly that he had not run from his discomfort but had stayed with it and felt it. I commended him for withstanding his painful situation but felt I needed to remind him of another reality. There is a danger that we may focus so totally on the negative elements in our lives that we live out of that place and it becomes our identity. We completely block out the greater and positive reality of who we are and what we possess in Christ.

The false-self

Our 'survival kits' are as strong and as stubbornly
maintained as we feel they need to be. For some unfortunate
children the need to build a strong impenetrable structure
around themselves has seemed a matter of life or death. This
is particularly the case for a child who has suffered a
significant amount of shaming. He believes himself to be
disgusting, a mistake, or in some way unacceptable. As a
result he will, almost unconsciously, construct a complex
structure to hide the now shame-based inner-self. 'Shame
is a kind of soul murder . . . Shame is a total non-self-
acceptance.' It differs from guilt. 'Guilt says I've done
something wrong; shame says there is something wrong with
me. Guilt says I've made a mistake; shame says I am a
mistake. Guilt says what I did was not good; shame says
I am no good.[2] No one can live with such feelings of
disgust about his real-self. In order to survive he will
fabricate a web of illusions so that no one will guess at the
truth. The false-self will bear no resemblance to the shamed
inner-self. The false-self will most likely appear very capable
and confident. The real truth must never be discovered by
anyone. The real truth can even be lost to the person himself
until uncovered indirectly through some unforeseen
happening or directly by revelation from God.

On several occasions I have watched a person first recoil
and then curl into a ball when, during a prayer counselling
time, God has shown him this shamed inner-part of himself.
First, he has recoiled from the truth and then he has tried
desperately to hide by covering up his inner-self with his own
body. It is a distressing sight. A person who has built up
a false-self around the real-self within will only mature
spiritually as that false-self is stripped off. David Benner
calls the false-self 'a neurotic encrustment around the spirit'.
One's false-self is a way of protecting oneself 'from
encounter with the deepest aspects of our being. . . . This

false self blocks us from growth and must be seen for what it is, a defence against the deeper experience of our true self and of life.'[3]I once had the disconcerting experience of trying to relate to a middle-aged man who for almost all his waking hours played the loveable clown. Every attempt at looking behind the mask was met with yet another joke. However, just occasionally in an unguarded moment, his eyes would cease their perpetual dance of merriment and become frighteningly empty. One wondered what pain necessitated the maintenance of such a false-self?

Dependency on other people (being 'bent towards the creature')

Possibly the most common way of controlling our fears and meeting our needs is through other people, as has been said. Most of us have dependency needs which are quite within normal limits. However, these needs should never dominate our lives. They should not determine our activities nor fill our thoughts. It should be within our capacity to express them or control them, whichever would be most appropriate at the time.

Unforgiveness

Another form of self-protection which needs to be relinquished is unforgiveness. The power of anger and bitterness protects us against feeling the depth of our pain. We fear that to release forgiveness would leave us unprotected against further hurt.

Past hurts cling tenaciously. Every memory of them revives the pain. When significant people in our lives, who profess to care, harm us by selfish and careless behaviour, it is hard to relinquish the hurt. On the occasions when the offender acknowledges his offence and asks for pardon we can usually forgive. More often than not, however, the person remains blissfully unaware of the harm he has done us and the idea that he should ask for our forgiveness never occurs to him. And yet Jesus insisted that His followers should forgive all those who sinned against them.

One dictionary definition of forgiveness is 'to pardon or cease to feel resentment against a person, to overlook a debt or trespass' (Chambers' *Everyday Dictionary*). How is this possible? To acknowledge the hurt and the painful feelings appropriately is the first step in the process. A young girl who had been sexually abused by her father as a child needed to express her feelings many times emphatically and emotionally in the presence of her counsellor before she was able to give up her desire to punish him. Appropriate expression of the bad feelings may be an important part of the healing process but at some point the releasing of forgiveness must begin.

Withholding forgiveness is a way of punishing the offender. Our sense of justice demands that sin be punished. If the sin is against us the inner cry for justice is even stronger. But being imperfect, fallible human beings we could never be absolutely fair in our judgment. Only God could be so just. Once we forgive others their sins against us we relinquish the right to punish. We hand judgment over to God.

The story of the unmerciful servant ends with him in prison suffering torment because he would not forgive his debtor. Jesus rounds the story off with the terrible words: 'This is how my heavenly Father will treat each of you unless you forgive your brother from your heart' (Matt.18:35). When we hold on to bitterness and resentment we ourselves become imprisoned by them. They act as chains preventing us from continuing on our journey. The 'tormentors' appear in the form of physical illness, emotional pain and spiritual decline. Recently I spoke to a middle-aged lady who had been greatly hurt by another Christian. I recognised that it was going to be a very difficult task for her to be able to forgive but I suggested that this would have to be a priority on her agenda. She looked doubtful, so I pressed my point, telling her the story of the unmerciful servant. I happened to suggest that sometimes the tormentors for us could be such things as arthritis, headaches, physical and emotional sickness. I was totally unaware that she suffered from any of these symptoms. She looked startled. Without a word she held up her hands which were already showing signs of a crippling arthritic condition.

Past hurts are sometimes hard to forgive but so too are past sins. It is sometimes difficult to forgive those who have sinned against us. It can also be difficult to forgive ourselves when we have sinned. Instead we live in continual guilt and condemnation. Unforgiveness towards self is a way of trying to make ourselves pay for our own sin. We punish ourselves and by so doing we deny the efficacy of Christ's sacrifice for us on the cross. Self-condemnation, misery and self-pity usually result.

Before the prodigal son could experience the warmth of his father's welcome and the wonderful celebration of his home-coming he had first to abandon the far country. This sort of exchange can only be fully experienced and enjoyed by those who manage to give up their old 'survival kit' and come empty-handed into their Heavenly Father's presence.

Steps to relinquishment and exchange

It is not an easy discipline and will need constant encouragement — it may only be achieved gradually. Nevertheless as we strive to leave behind the old 'survival kit' we will discover several indispensable stages in the process.

Recognition

The prodigal 'came to his senses'. It was a moment of realisation. Before we can begin moving towards maturity in any significant way there needs to be this flash of clarity. It comes to us all in different ways. Perhaps it is just an awareness that one's life lacks direction and is going nowhere. It could be the sudden revelation that one's goals are all selfishly motivated. Maybe like the prodigal we find ourselves in a place of life-threatening crisis.

In her book *Puppet on a String*, Helena Wilkinson describes her fight with 'anorexia nervosa'. The moment of crisis came one night in hospital. She describes it: 'I felt that the little life within me was being drained from my body and the hands of Death were firmly gripping me. I had no more strength to fight, no will to live. All I could do was pray to God that His will for me should be done. At that moment I just surrendered to Him the little life that was left and said, 'Lord, if you want me to die, I'll die, but if you want me to live then give me the courage to fight this illness and live.'' [4] From that instant improvement began. Helena still had a long, arduous journey ahead but it started with that flash of frightening insight into her real predicament.

Repentance

Recognition will bring the same reaction as the prodigal's: 'I have sinned.' 'I have gone my own way. I have forsaken God. I have tried to meet my needs through my own devices.'

Frequently we by-pass the need for full repentance for the ungodly attitudes and the self-centred goals that have dominated our lives. We hope the healing will come without this painful process. Repentance is foundational to Christian healing and Christian counsellors cannot by-pass the need for it.

Leanne Payne writes of the error that affects so many Christian ministers. She calls it 'psychologising' the Gospel. 'Thinking only of the person's emotional needs and the current wisdom for meeting them, the modern minister forgets to invoke the Presence of God and call down upon the needy person the grace to repent. He has neglected the root healing, out of which all ongoing progress comes . . . To be a Christian minister is to call the needy to a radical and full repentance, and then, in the power of the Spirit, to proclaim forgiveness in such a way that the repentant one can receive it.'[5]

Struggle and risk

Godly sorrow for one's sin facilitates change. As the conviction grows that one is not living in a godly fashion, so too does the desire to change. However the struggle to 'give up' the old and 'take up' the new will always be an element in this discipline. Part of the struggle will be facing our inner pain and waiting for God to come to our rescue.

Frank Lake tells the story of a client whose hysterical need for company forced him to plan his life so carefully that he was never alone. Eventually he challenged his own anxiety and deliberately refused to take his normal escape route. Although it created a great panic within him he stayed with his 'aloneness' and cried out to God for help. After about half-an-hour there came over him a tremendous sense of warmth and of another presence. He knew he need never be afraid in that way again. For the first time in his life he had gone deliberately right through, and into, that place of terror, and out the other side.[6]

The only way we will ever discover if God is able to meet us in our deepest need is when we forgo our normal escape routes and risk the emptiness, the pain, the panic and find Him right there, as the psalmist did: 'Where can I go from your Spirit? Where can I flee from your presence? . . . If I make my bed in the depths, you are there' (Ps.139:7,8).

Laying aside a habitually used identity is not an easy task. In my experience it will need to be worked at on a daily basis before the habit is broken. All my life I have adopted a strong 'I don't need anyone' image. The laying aside of this has taken time and effort. First I had to recognise its existence and then to see it for what it really was — a way of meeting my needs for significance and value. I needed some friends to help me unravel the roots of this identity and also their prayers to help me renounce my irrational belief — that it was best to be strong and not to need other people. Having done all this, I still had to relinquish the old behaviour pattern and exchange it for something more Christ-like.

Just the other morning I met an acquaintance who politely enquired after my health. Immediately, and without thinking, I replied that I was quite well. It was a habitual response but immediately I felt uneasy. I had not spoken the truth. In fact my back was quite painful and I was having a job coping with normal life. Quickly I changed my reply and said that although I was pretty well my back was playing up. This laying down of my old response proved very beneficial to me because my friend gave me the name of the physiotherapist who gave me such excellent advice on how to take responsibility for looking after my back. Almost daily I have the choice between the old identity, which gives very little away and the new one which is more open and vulnerable. I hope the new is making me more approachable and human!

The struggle to push through pain and to 'let go' familiar patterns will mark the practice of this discipline but sooner or later our struggles must be accompanied by an act of faith as we 'give up' the familiar and hope that the exchange will have been worth the risk. R-I-S-K — I remember once hearing John Wimber say that that was how the word 'faith' was spelt! R-I-S-K. The prodigal took a risk. His father might never have received him back as a son. All he had to hold on to was the memory of a father who had been merciful and generous. Trusting in that he made his way homewards.

Helena Wilkinson, mentioned above, could not be sure that God would meet her needs. But she stepped out and took the risk. 'I had spent my time searching for love and security in the things I did, and more especially in the people I met. My endless searching was to no avail.' She had tried to find her security apart from God. She had to take the risk of relinquishing her unhealthy methods for meeting her needs and trust that God alone would provide for her. Soon after this she read some words from the Bible which leapt out at her − 'God is love' (1 John 4:16). She had discovered a vital secret: 'a love that would never let me down'.[7] Gradually she began to experience God's capacity to meet her needs. The more she surrendered to God the more He was able to satisfy and fulfil her.

Balancing

Struggle and risk will be essential steps in the practice of this discipline. So too will be finding a balance. The danger of imbalance or over-reaction is present every time we leave one position and take up a new one. This is true whether it is a child moving from one stage of development to the next or an adult leaving one job for another.

As we seek to change unhealthy and ungodly behaviour patterns the same tendency will be present, unless we work at finding a balance. The inflexible, controlling adult needs to become more spontaneous and free. But not to the extent that the normal responsibilities of life are ignored. The independent, strong woman needs to allow for normal weakness and to become more inter-dependent. At first she may experience overwhelming dependency needs and the next moment swing away into total denial of such feelings. Finding a balance may be a long process.

A young girl received counselling because of an overwhelming fear of men. During the course of counselling she realised that part of her normal self-protective mechanism seemed to be missing — she never felt angry. She was a past-master at suppression and had in fact buried many of her feelings. Gradually she laid down her habit of suppression and began to discover 'new' emotions, one of which was anger. Soon after this discovery she found herself in an awkward position. She was approached by an over-friendly young man who was a little the worse for drink. When he did not immediately take 'no' for an answer she became very angry and quite inappropriately hit out at him extremely hard. Her newfound feelings had not yet stabilised.

When we relinquish familiar patterns of behaviour for unfamiliar ones it is not always easy to find the correct balance. We may need some help from friends and we certainly need help from God.

Another helper

'The Lord is with me; I will not be afraid . . . he is my helper' (Ps.118:6,7). The hard task of 'letting go' is sometimes a long and painful procedure or sometimes a relatively quick one. However it may be, we cannot accomplish it alone. Jesus knew this when He promised His disciples another counsellor. 'I will ask the Father, and he will give you another Counsellor to be with you for ever . . . Do not let your hearts be troubled and do not be afraid' (John 14:16,27).

Paul was joyfully confident that once God had started His work He would finish it. '. . . being am confident of this, that he who began a good work in you will carry it on to completion until the day of Christ Jesus' (Phil.1:6).

With God's help we will be able to relinquish our self-made 'survival kits'; and our self-indulgent goals. Then the great exchange can take place. God will bind up the broken hearts, fill the empty spaces and satisfy the deepest longings.

We once prayed with a man who had suffered terrible

shaming as a child. Whenever we drew near to pray with him he would demonstrate the distressing type of symptom that I have mentioned before. He would cower in his chair and then curl up as if to protect his inner-self from being seen. Every session the same thing occurred until one day quite spontaneously our prayers changed to worship. Gradually he began to join in and we praised together for about ten minutes. The room seemed to fill with the glory of God. When we eventually looked up, our friend was sitting bolt upright with his arms raised towards Heaven. When we focus on God, the healing of the inner-self begins and we no longer need the protection of 'survival kits' or false-selves. They can then be relinquished.

The prodigal son left the far country, exchanging it for his father's presence. This exchange forms the basis for our final discipline. It is as we enjoy the presence of God that we become whole. But it takes discipline to maintain this important relationship.

Exercises

1. Share with your group/friend/journal a childhood experience of relinquishment and exchange.

2. When you first became a Christian was there something you had to give up? Was this difficult or easy?

3. Are you inclined to use any of the methods of control mentioned? If so share what this does for you.

4. Write in your journal your own name and beside it any special identity you have (e.g., Susan, the mistake!). Ask God to show you who you are in His sight and write that down. Now write down the names of your group and ask God to give you a special name for each one of them, e.g., Mary, 'my servant', or Nick, 'my chosen one'.

5. Share these names with the group. Add the names the others give to you to the one God has already shown you. Keep this as a constant reminder of your true identity.

6. Write in your journal two headings — 'Relinquishment' and 'Exchange'. Under the first write anything you know that still needs to be relinquished. Perhaps it is something you have become aware of whilst reading this chapter or doing the exercises. Wait on God to show you what He will exchange this for. E.g.:

Relinquishment	*Exchange*
Getting my value from my job	Sonship
Security from relationships	My promise never to leave you

7. End by praying that each will be given the courage to continue the struggle over relinquishment.

10. CELEBRATING THE FATHER'S PRESENCE

' "Bring the fattened calf and kill it. Let's have a feast and celebrate" ' (Luke 15:23).

The prodigal son slunk painfully home, his inheritance spent, his friends gone, his physical strength exhausted. In fact all his normal devices for getting his needs met had failed. He had been compelled to relinquish every one of them. He was still a distance from his home when his father saw him and ran to meet him. The warmth of his father's welcome surprised and overwhelmed him. Then almost before he could take it all in he was swept into an extravagant celebration.

All this marked the beginning of a new relationship between father and son. After the celebrations the relationship would need to be explored, developed and maintained.

Learning to celebrate the Father's presence is the most important discipline of all and if there was a right order it would take priority. However, although it may be the most important, it is impossible to truly celebrate His presence without at least attempting the other disciplines. We may regularly come into His presence, rather like the older brother, but the intimacy and blessing of an unclouded relationship will elude us.

As we consider this discipline we will first notice the different factors which made the initial celebration possible.

Next the older brother's reaction will cause us to look at some of the things which could prevent us enjoying God's presence. Then we will examine ways in which we can encourage the daily practice of celebration after the initial party is over. Last, to spur us on, we will look at the benefits of implementing this discipline.

Necessary prior factors

The son came home knowing from hard experience that his own methods of survival were deficient. He came empty-handed. He came with no personal resources. He came like a small child dependent on his father. That was exactly what Jesus meant us to be like when He said, 'Unless you change and become like little children, you will never enter the kingdom of heaven' (Matt. 18:3). This is the first requirement for celebration.

Child-likeness

We must recognise that the 'survival kits' we have constructed, the false selves we have built and the selfish ambitions we have held, are totally inadequate and will never heal the inner pain or meet our needs. When we lay them down our 'inner-child' is free to come out of hiding. We become dependent, vulnerable, spontaneous, trusting – the right attitude to receive the father's love and mercy.

At a recent conference in New Zealand I had been speaking on the dysfunctional family when I stressed the importance of the father's rôle in affirming a daughter's sexuality. At the end of the session I invited any women present who had never had their femininity affirmed by their father to come forward to receive prayer. The thought suddenly crossed my mind that there might also be a few men present who could need a similar sort of prayer. Rather hesitantly, I suggested that any men who had never experienced their father's affirmation should come forward and my husband, David, would pray for them. I expected three or four men to come forward but instead a line began to form which grew and grew. These great, tall New Zealanders humbled themselves and became like little children. The tears poured down their faces as they waited. Many of them sobbed in David's arms as he prayed for them. It was a most moving sight. As Carlo Carretto unhesitatingly affirms: 'A serious beginning is made in the spiritual life the moment a man makes a genuine act of humility'.[1]

When we become like 'little children' the Father greets us with His arms open wide. 'This son of mine who was dead in his sinful ways is alive,' He will say. 'The child who was lost beneath the false-self is found. Let us have a feast and celebrate.'

The practice of the other disciplines

Child-likeness alone is not sufficient to enable a person to fully enjoy the Father's presence. A disciplined life-style is also required. So often we have watched counsellees struggling with one of the disciplines and known that until it is mastered they will never have the freedom to celebrate with real joy.

The discipline that gives rise to the greatest joy is that of relinquishment and exchange. The ability to relinquish whatever was asked of him was exactly what the rich young ruler lacked. Jesus said to him, 'Sell your possessions and give to the poor, and you will have treasure in heaven. Then come, follow me' (Matt.19:21). This young ruler was evidently an upright, law-abiding person. It seemed that he was probably observing all the disciplines we have mentioned except this one – how could he relinquish the thing that gave him so much prestige, comfort and pleasure? He could not be certain that the exchange would be as prestigious or as comfortable or as pleasurable. He went away very sad, having forfeited the privilege of keeping company with Jesus.

I once ministered to two people separately. They had been in a wrong sexual relationship together. The girl blamed the man and was full of reasons as to why she was a victim rather than a responsible party in the relationship. She continued in hurt and blame and seemed unable to find any healing. The man, on the other hand, came to see me in a totally different frame of mind. He took full responsibility, was deeply ashamed of his immorality and repented in tears. In contrast to the girl, he found forgiveness, healing and freedom to enjoy God's presence once again.

The prodigal son's return to his father demonstrates genuine relinquishment. In his first words to his father he put his needs to one side and poured out a confession. In so doing he showed that his first priority was to take responsibility for himself and he did not avoid communicating painful truth about his own sinfulness. He must in fact have been exhausted and footsore as well as starving, but he made no emotional appeal, nor gave excuses. He simply said, 'Father, I have sinned against heaven and against you. I am no longer worthy to be called your son' (Luke 15:21). We are also told that he was willing to lose his status as son and become like one of his father's hired hands (verse 19). He had the desire to change. The relinquishment of the old patterns had already begun.

The son had come back to his father with a broken-down life. His father gave him a brand-new start, and gave him far more than he deserved. As the father called for a ring to be put on his son's finger he publicly acknowledged him as his son and reinstated him. At that moment the son's state of slavery was exchanged for sonship. Then he provided a robe to cover the young man's rags and tatters. He clothed him in 'garments of salvation' and arrayed him in 'a robe of righteousness' (Is.61:10). Sin and shame were exchanged for cleansing and covering. The father then called the servants to bring a pair of sandals. His feet were washed and freshly shod. Weariness and pain were exchanged for refreshment and healing.

If a person is full of anxiety, or fear, or guilt there is no way he or she can enter into the joy of celebration until these things are dealt with. On one occasion a young woman came to me after an evening service and asked for prayer. She looked very unhappy and told me the tragic story of her teenage rebellion which had resulted in two aborted pregnancies. She felt that God would never forgive her. Her guilt weighed her down and was sapping her enjoyment of life. She felt there was nothing to live for. I tried to explain that if we repent and confess our sins 'he is faithful and just and will forgive us our sins' (1 John 1:9). But it seemed to make no difference to her. Eventually I suggested that she closed her eyes and stretched out her hands. I told her to imagine transferring her sins to her outstretched hands. With her cupped hands still held in front of her I led her to an enormous cross which was suspended on the back wall of the church. I explained that I wanted her to place her hands on the foot of the cross and that as she did so she was to envisage her sins being laid upon the cross. I then told her that when she was ready she could take her hands off, but when she did so she should leave her sins on the cross and she was never to pick them up again. They were where they belonged. For quite a long time she stood before the cross with her hands resting on it. With a great sigh she took her hands away and in that instant fell to her knees and began to cry. She wept and wept. I prayed that God would minister His forgiveness and peace to her heart. In between the sobs she kept saying, 'Thank you Jesus. Thank you Jesus.' She had exchanged her sins for God's mercy. It was a wonderful experience simply to behold her joy.

To return to the prodigal: as if the ring, the robe and the sandals were not enough, the father called for a celebration. 'Kill the fatted calf. Let's have a feast and celebrate.' It was an incredible party with music, dancing, singing, clapping and shouting for joy; a celebration the son could never have imagined even in his wildest dreams. Now he could identify with King David's song:

> 'You turned my wailing into dancing; you removed my sackcloth and clothed me with joy, that my heart may sing to you and not be silent.' (Psalm 30:11–12).

Despair and mourning were exchanged for praise and gladness.

Several years ago I attended a conference at Wembley led by John Wimber. One evening after a number of prophecies there was a time of weeping and repenting which lasted quite a time. When this had finished John Wimber rose to speak. However, he had only got as far as reading out his text when someone began to laugh, then another person, and another, and another. Gradually the laughter spread around almost the whole of that vast centre. A large man fell backwards off his chair and a young man rocked and rolled down the aisle. John watched for a while and then announced to everyone that God was throwing a party. He brought the musicians back on the stage and for the next hour we danced, sang and clapped; a young girl even did cartwheels around the balcony! We celebrated the Father's presence at His invitation and initiation.

A revelation of the father's character

Another cause for the son's joy must have been a fresh insight into his father's character. Our Heavenly Father is unlike any earthly father. Those with distorted views of God which they may have gained through past teaching or personal experience with their own fathers would do well to study this story.

What we see here is a father — *par excellence*. The father spied his son in the distance. This was hardly a casual glance out of the window coinciding with his son's appearance on the sky-line. The father had been on the look-out for his son's return since the day he first left. The father had endured the pain of separation and he was determined to wait for his boy's return, however long it took. 'For the Lord is good and his love endures for ever; his faithfulness continues through all generations' (Ps.100:5). He was actually waiting to welcome his wayward child. 'Yet the Lord longs to be gracious to you; he rises to show you compassion' (Is 30:18).

Even whilst the son was a long way off the father recognised him. He knew his son's walk very well. He had maybe helped the toddler take his first faltering steps. He had probably watched his young boy running around the fields. Later he might have observed those dragging footsteps coming in from work. Finally, did he follow the figure of his youngest son as he faded away into the distance? Surely time and love had etched that walk on the father's memory. There is nothing about us the Father does not know. Jesus said, 'I am the good shepherd; I know my sheep and my sheep know me' (John 10:14). Our Heavenly Father knows us intimately. Even our tears are measured on His scroll (Ps.56:8) and each single hair upon our heads is numbered (Luke 12:7).

The story of the prodigal son is the only place in the Bible where we see God in a hurry. It was as if for him nothing else in the world mattered. The day's business, the sun's heat, the lowering of his dignity, the son's betrayal, were all forgotten. Only embracing his boy and having him home again was important. A broken-down, disappointed and repentant sinner had returned. Even from a distance the father could read the boy's heart. He knew that his son had

finally faced reality; both that of the world and of his own
heart. Compassion was the father's response. This is always
God's response to His children when they come back. Never
for an instant have they been out of His thoughts. He has
longed after them as a mother yearns over her children. But,
says God, even if a mother should forget her suckling babe,
yet, 'I will not forget you! See, I have engraved you on the
palms of my hands' (Is.49:15,16).

Generosity poured from the father. He held nothing
back. It was no formal handshake nor stiff embrace
which welcomed the son. He was completely oblivious
to others as he expressed his love and joy. Running!
Embracing! Kissing! What an amazing picture of God
our Heavenly Father! Indeed He has loved us 'with an
everlasting love', He has 'drawn' us 'with loving-kindness'
(Jer.31:3).

Many of us picture God as solemn and awesome. And
that's true. But there are times when God is joyful. When
one sinner repents all Heaven rejoices. The Father knows
how to celebrate. The boy had left home to find pleasure
and excitement. But when he experienced them he found
them to be false and empty. But he knew he had the real
thing in his father's house. 'You will fill me with joy in your
presence, with eternal pleasures at your right hand'
(Ps.16:11).

The party was already under-way when the older brother
returned from work and heard music and dancing. His
reaction to the situation was a common one: he became
angry and sulked. He refused to join in the fun. Although
the older brother had remained at home physically he had
evidently drifted as far from his father's presence
emotionally and spiritually as his younger brother had done.
He also therefore, needed to make a journey back, because
conditions existed in his life which effectively blocked the
enjoyment of his father's presence. He does not seem to have
realised it but he too needed to practise the disciplines of

relinquishment and exchange if the obstacles were to be removed.

Factors which prevent celebration

Many people suffer from that 'older brother' syndrome and live with the same distaste of celebration which was operating in his life.

Bad feelings

Uncomfortable feelings are difficult to handle and get in the way of our enjoyment of God. It was the older brother's anger which prevented him from joining in the party. As already stated, anger is a secondary emotion. People are not angry without cause, although the cause may be buried in the unconscious. Usually anger sits on hurt – real or perceived. The older brother expressed resentment and jealousy of his younger brother, which points to unresolved issues from his past. Numerous times I have prayed with men and women who struggle with unresolved emotional problems involving a brother or sister. The jealousy or resentment has smouldered deep down, causing depression, feelings of self-pity and even sudden outbursts of rage. Until the original hurt is uncovered, and with God's help resolved, there will be no healing. The person remains bound by the bad feelings which sap the sparkle and enjoyment of life.

Immaturity

An immature self-centredness is another factor that prevents one engaging in celebration. The older brother was well past the narcissistic teenage years, yet he still showed that immature tendency towards self-centredness. He was so sorry for himself: 'You never gave *me* even a young goat so I could celebrate with my friends' (Luke 15:29). Self-pity is an insidious trap which sucks a person down deeper and deeper into a bottomless pit. Grief is healing. Self-pity is Satan's counterfeit. Those who have indulged in it for too long have found themselves dominated and gripped by it. Self-pity locks us into self-consciousness, whereby we only notice ourselves and how we are feeling. We miss seeing the many beautiful, pleasurable and lovely things around. Other people's lives are of no interest. Their happiness and their problems go unnoticed by us.

I once met a lady whose life was dominated by self-pity. She talked non-stop about a hurt she had received years ago. She could never leave the subject and if temporarily side-tracked always returned to it, like a dog to a bone. The wellbeing and happiness of her family did not seem to concern her. When her children eventually left home, she complained that they never visited her. They for their part, had no desire to visit a woman whose self-pity had filled their childhood with gloom.

The older brother's self-righteousness was another sign of immaturity. 'All these years I've been slaving for you and never disobeyed your orders' (Luke 15:29), he said, as he complained of his younger brother's wild behaviour. He saw himself as far superior. He congratulated himself on never breaking the letter of the law. However, Jesus said that the most important commandment was to 'love the Lord your God with all your heart and with all your soul and with all your mind and with all your strength. The second is this: Love your neighbour as yourself. There is no commandment greater than these' (Mark 12:30,31). An immature person takes only shallow glimpses into his own heart. He avoids situations which could cause him to search more deeply. He is unfamiliar with such prayers as David's for God to search and know his heart (Ps.139:23).

Distorted perceptions

The older brother's irrational beliefs were another factor which kept him from the party. He was holding some very twisted ideas which must have affected his feelings and his behaviour. 'Look! All these years I've been slaving for you. . .' (Luke 15:29). He saw himself as a slave not a son. He viewed his father as a hard slave-driver, not as a loving parent. Whilst he saw himself and his father in these distorted terms he would continue to be angry and resentful and to feel self-righteous and sorry for himself. He would have an excuse not to celebrate – slaves are not allowed to think of enjoying life.

The father's response to the older brother was to speak the truth to him. 'You are always with me and everything I have is yours' (Luke 15:31). We can almost see the father shaking his head in disbelief that his eldest son could not accept the truth. Every moment of every day the older brother had had access to his father's presence. His son and heir had always been free to enjoy every single thing the father owned. But he had not learned how to celebrate any of this.

Distorted attitudes will affect our approach to other people and life in general. They will keep us from celebrating anything. The older brother had believed a lie and only his father could help him to discern the true from the false.

Celebrating the Father's presence on a daily basis

Once the welcome-home party was over the younger brother would have needed to settle down and learn how to enjoy his father's presence on a daily basis. So too must we. There are the high points in our lives when celebration flows naturally and easily from our hearts. However, most of us live rather humdrum existences and during such ordinary times we also need to learn how to appreciate and enjoy God's presence. A commitment to practise certain spiritual disciplines will help us.

Consciously acknowledging God's presence

Practising the presence of God, writes Leanne Payne, is: 'simply the discipline of calling to mind the truth that God is with us.'[2] It is a deliberate policy of remembering that He is here.

When I was a very new Christian I went to see my rector with, what to my mind, was an insoluble problem. Before becoming a Christian I had agreed to attend a party with a boy friend. I did not want to let him down at the last minute but now I felt uncomfortable at going to, what I knew from experience, would be a very godless, even immoral, event. My rector was a wise man. 'Well Mary,' he said, 'why don't you take Jesus with you to the party?' I was filled with amazement and awe at such a suggestion. However, I took his advice and went to the party, having first invited Jesus to be with me. My boy friend was puzzled by the change in me. On hearing my explanation, he insisted we left immediately. He said that he didn't feel comfortable having Jesus in such a place!

I have always been grateful that I was given such good counsel at the beginning of my Christian life. At first it is not easy to remember and one has to adopt a deliberate policy of practising the presence of God. It gradually becomes a natural habit. Similarly when a person first gets married it is hard to think in terms of two people. Conversely the longer one is married the harder it is to revert to thinking in terms of one person again.

Deliberate communication with God

We also inspire celebration when we commune with Him.

One of the best ways of conversing with God is by using a two-way journal. Our thoughts tend to wander less when we write our prayers down and we are inclined to listen more carefully when we are waiting to record God's response to our prayers. Under these conditions our communication becomes a two-way conversation with God instead of a one-way shopping-list.

God also communicates through silence. Communication is far more than words. 'Words, words, words. They form the floor, the walls and the ceiling of our existence.'[3] So writes Henri Nouwen in an attempt to encourage his readers to hear the Word of God born out of the eternal silence of God. ' . . . and it is to this Word out of silence that we want to be witnesses.'[4]

Solitude and silence can be frightening experiences to the modern man, born into a noise-saturated society. Jesus frequently needed to be alone. At the beginning of His ministry he spent forty days alone in the desert. Subsequently He often withdrew to silent, lonely places to be with His Father. Christians need to seek times, as Jesus did, to be alone with God. This is what Richard Foster calls 'the recreating stillness of solitude'.[5] Yet rather than seek it, many of us fill our moments of solitude with activity and noise, fearing the emptiness we could experience without it. 'Loneliness is inner emptiness. Solitude is inner fulfilment,' writes Foster. And again 'If we possess inward solitude we will not fear being alone.'[6] The only way of overcoming the terrible fear of loneliness and discovering the fulfilment of solitude is to challenge and stay with the loneliness until God meets us in it and the emptiness is filled with His presence.

Some years ago a member of our staff at St Andrew's, the Rev. Barry Kissell, decided he needed to cultivate the discipline of spending one day a week in solitude listening to God. Initially he encountered many difficulties. At first the time crept by, his mind 'rotated like a merry-go-round', he fell asleep, and was even assailed with fear and wanted to leave his garden retreat. He decided that this solitude and stillness was something that only especially dedicated people were able to endure and benefit from. However, despite the difficulties, he persevered. Now God meets him in the solitude. 'At the Grail I sit quietly and seek the Lord, and find that He comes to me in non-verbal ways. It is as if His Spirit touches my spirit and at times I sing or dance for joy.'[7]

Solitude and silence pay good dividends. The 'gentle whisper' of God is heard in the silence. So often we read the word of God and acknowledge its truth. We read that God loves us, that we are of value and worth to Him. We know that He promises comfort and guidance and yet, this knowledge, in many instances, never changes our feelings or our behaviour. We still seek our value and security from elsewhere; anxiety and fear are frequent companions. The truth of God's Word seems not to have penetrated into our innermost beings. It is as we cultivate solitude and silence that we begin to hear God with our inner-ear. How often we have mistakenly assumed that God was more present to us in the large noisy gatherings. It was when Elijah fled in fear to a lonely place that he heard God again. This time in a 'gentle whisper'. Elijah did not hear him in the wind, the earthquake or the fire (1 Kings 19:12).

Acknowledging our position as God's children

It seems that the older son had never spent much time communicating with his father. Nor had he appreciated the meaning of sonship.

'Everything I have is yours' (Luke 15:31), said the father to his son. Everything means everything! His cattle, his land, his house, his servants, his food, his mercy, his love, his forgiveness, his power – on and on . . . Everything was there for his sons to appreciate and delight in. Wasn't that enough to celebrate? The older son had obviously never begun to experience life as his father's heir. He had thought like a servant, felt like a servant and behaved like a servant, when in reality he was a dearly loved son who was free to enjoy the benefits of his father's wealth.

After the festivities were over the younger son would also have to grow accustomed to living from his position of sonship. He had been a hired servant in the far country with no privileges. Most likely he had worked there with reluctance and with bad grace. Now everything had changed and he would have to learn how to live, work and play as a son. He had to learn to walk in the stature, security and freedom of sonship. He must neither abuse it, nor take it for granted, nor fail to appreciate the wonder of it, as the older brother had done.

When life has been painful and people who should have known better have proved untrustworthy, it is very easy to assume the role of the perpetual victim. The temptation is to live our life from that hurting position. At some stage we must take the risk of forsaking that familiar rôle and accepting our position as true sons of God.

The cattle on a thousand hills belong to God (Ps.50:10). We are His heirs – heirs of God and joint-heirs with Christ (Rom.8:17). Let us then appreciate the Father's invitation to enjoy His company and His 'everything'.

The benefits of celebrating the Father's presence

A daily celebration of God's presence brings its own rewards.

We gain a true perspective on life

'I would say that it is precisely in prayer that you learn to recognise more clearly than ever your own limitations, your measure as a created, not a creating being, the radical powerlessness of your poverty. And you will experience this above all if you have the courage to make your way in faith to the frontiers of the invisible.'[8]

Growing up within easy reach of the Atlantic Ocean I soon learned a healthy respect for the great 'white horses'. That was our name for the huge rollers at Westward Ho! that smashed against the sea wall in the winter storms. I sensed my own weakness in the face of such a merciless force. I did not need my mother's repeated warnings nor a sighting of the red flag to make me careful. The sight of those huge 'white horses' was all I needed. Even the sound of their presence was sufficient.

As we dwell in the presence of Almighty God His infinite greatness stands out in contrast to our finite smallness. In His presence we gain a true perspective on life. We are but dust and our days like grass or a wild flower (Psalm 103:14—15) — here today and gone tomorrow. We are created beings who only have significance in relationship to our Creator. Only as we recognise His worth do we discover our own. As we look into His eyes our aching heart is comforted. He is the one who 'fills everything in every way' (Eph.1:23).

It is also in the light of God's love that we can relax about ourselves. For too much of our time we find ourselves taking centre stage in our own thoughts. We are prevented from taking ourselves too seriously once we have learned to celebrate God's presence continually. We are also delivered from becoming stuffy bores. 'Of all people we should be the most free, alive, interesting. Celebration adds a note of gaiety, festivity, hilarity to our lives.'[9]

We are made whole

Another benefit is personal wholeness. Healing comes as this discipline is practised. Being in the daily presence of a Father who values and loves us makes the once needed 'survival kit' superfluous. 'It is in this worship that our one true face appears, displacing the old false faces. It is in this honest and open speaking relationship that our true self bursts forth, cracking the shell of the old false self; and our old bondages and compulsions fall away with it.'[10]

Grace Sheppard contended for many years with fear. Writing so honestly about her struggles it is clear that she had put into practice the disciplines we have mentioned in these chapters, not least this important discipline of practising God presence. She writes, 'Where, finally, can we find the strength to master our fears, to achieve wholeness? There is a place . . . This place is the Throne of Grace. It is where God is, and is a place of prayer. I believe that God is with us, firmly rooted, in the whole of creation, and in each other. Finding ways of meeting Him in simple communication, we shall find we are loved, and healed and, inch by inch, delivered from the grip of our fears.'[11]

We straighten up from our bent position

It is only in Him that we become persons . . . He calls the real 'I' forward, separating us from our sicknesses and sins. We then no longer define ourselves by our sins, neuroses, and deprivations, but by Him whose healing life cleanses and indwells us. From being bent torwards the creature – the horizontal position of the Fall – we straighten up into the completing union with the Creator – the vertical, listening position of the free creature.[12]

Leanne Payne tells the story of Patsy Casey, one of her fellow workers. Patsy was the product of a very dysfunctional family and consequently had some deep emotional wounds for which she needed professional help. Frequently she would live from the immature, hurting centre of the 'wounded child'. During these times she would be angry with everyone, with the Church, even with God. Eventually Leanne found the key to help her. She told Patsy that one of the big differences between them was that when she hurt she would stand up straight and hurt, praying until God sent help. It might take a while, but eventually help would come. She explained to Patsy that she had grown up in a home where, no matter what the suffering, her mother would stand without anger or self-pity, face upward towards God, ready to wait like that until kingdom come if necessary. Eventually Patsy learned to do this and Leanne comments, 'If ever one's wounds have been turned into healing power for others, Patsy Casey's have.'[13]

We will be changed into His likeness

As we practise the discipline of celebrating our Father's presence the most amazing transformation will begin to take place. We will become like the one we worship and with whom we spend our daily lives. 'Those who look to him are radiant' (Ps.34:5). 'And we, who with unveiled faces all reflect the Lord's glory, are being transformed into his likeness with ever-increasing glory, which comes from the Lord, who is the Spirit' (2 Cor.3:18).

It is often noticeable that a married couple who have spent many years together grow to be like one another. They become similar in their mannerisms. They will often think alike. One says something only to find the other about to say the same thing. As we consciously and deliberately practise God's presence we will find that little by little we are changed into the likeness of Jesus.

Paul considered everything a loss compared to the surpassing greatness of knowing Christ Jesus his Lord (Phil.3:8). This is true maturity – to know Jesus and to become like Him.

'Let us be among those who believe that the inner transformation of our lives is a goal worthy of our best effort.'[14]

Exercises

1. Immaturity prevents us fully enjoying our Heavenly Father's presence but child-likeness facilitates it. A child-like person is real, vulnerable, spontaneous, open and trusting. Which of these adjectives most describes you? Share this with your group/friend and see if they agree.

Which adjective least describes you? Share this with your group/friend, explaining the reason why you are not . . . e.g., 'I am not trusting because I fear being let down.'

2. Together compile a list of reasons you have for celebrating God's presence.

3. Once again read from pp. 148–9, 'a revelation of the Father's character'. Then close your eyes and take a few minutes to picture the whole scene. Meditate for another few minutes on one aspect of God's character which particularly moves you. When you are ready, share your experience with the group/friend.

4. Paul suggests we fill our minds with that which is true, noble, right, pure, lovely, admirable, excellent and praiseworthy (Phil.4:8). Jesus told us to consider the birds of the air and the lilies of the field (Matt.6:26,28). The creation should encourage us to trust our Heavenly Father's care for us.

Find a leaf, bud, plant, twig, a stone or some other part of God's creation and pass it around the group for a few minutes. Study its beauty and perfection.

Read aloud Psalm 147 (verses 7–11), Psalm 136 (verses 3–9) and Psalm 139 (verses 13–18). Now close your eyes and picture the immensity of the sun that shines by day, the clouds in the sky, the green grass wet with dew and rain, the cattle on the hills, the variety of birds chirping and singing in the garden. Then picture the night sky lit by the moon and hundreds of little stars.

From the grandeur of God's world slowly bring your mind
to focus on the culminating glory of His creation — a baby
forming in its mother's womb. You were once that baby;
fearfully and wonderfully made. Let your mind wander
through the years of your life. Each day has been ordained
by God. Gradually bring your mind to focus on this present
moment. 'When I awake I am still with you' (Ps.139:18).
Spend these last moments being aware and enjoying your
Heavenly Father's presence with you.

REFERENCES

Chapter 1

1. Leanne Payne, *The Broken Image*, Crossway Books, Illinois, 1981, p.139.
2. Grace Sheppard, *An Aspect of Fear*, Darton, Longman & Todd, London, 1989, p.61.
3. Bryce Courtenay, *The Power of One*, Random House, New York, 1989, p.2.
4. Richard F. Lovelace, *Dynamics of Spiritual Life*, Paternoster Press, Exeter, 1979, p.88.
5. Ibid., p.92.
6. C.S. Lewis, *The Great Divorce*, Fount Paperbacks, Collins, Glasgow, 1977, p.89.

Chapter 2

1. Richard Foster, *Celebration of Discipline*, Hodder & Stoughton, London, 1980, p.9.
2. Ibid., p.6.
3. John Powell & Loretta Brady, *Will the Real Me Please Stand Up?*, Tabor Pub., Valencia, CA, 1985, p.10.
4. C.S. Lewis, *The Great Divorce*, p.66.
5. John Powell & Loretta Brady, op. cit., p.23.

Chapter 3

1. Hugo F. Reading, *A Dictionary of the Social Sciences*, Routledge & Kegan Paul, London, 1977.

2. Dr. M. Scott Peck, *The Road Less Travelled*, Simon & Schuster, New York, 1978 p.24.
3. Barbara Gordon, *I'm Dancing as Fast as I Can*, Bantam Books, New York, 1979, p.163.
4. Trula Michaels LaCalle, Ph.D., *Voices*, Berkley Books, New York, 1989, p.166.
5. *The Sower Magazine*, Spring, 1989.

Chapter 4

1. John Powell & Loretta Brady, *Will the Real Me Please Stand Up?*, p.44.
2. Ibid., p.50.
3. Frank Lake (abridged M.H. Yeomans), *Clinical Theology*, Darton, Longman & Todd, London, 1986, pp.143,144,156.
4. John Powell & Loretta Brady, op.cit., p.46.
5. John Powell, *Happiness is an Inside Job*, Tabor Pub., Valencia, CA, 1989, p.3.
6. C.S. Lewis, *The Great Divorce*, p.21.
7. Ibid., p.8.
8. Frank Lake, op.cit., p.157.
9. John Powell, *Happiness is an Inside Job*, p.5.
10. John Powell, *The Christian Vision*, Argus Comms, Valencia, CA, 1984, p.15.

Chapter 5

1. Margaret Magdalen, *Transformed by Love*, Darton, Longman & Todd, London, 1989, p.15.
2. Ibid., p.7.
3. Charles Kraft, *Christianity With Power*, Vine Books, Servant Pubs, Michigan, 1989, p.92.
4. Leanne Payne, *The Healing Presence*, Crossway Books, Illinois, 1989, p.64.
5. David Benner, *Psychotherapy and the Spiritual Quest*, Hodder & Stoughton, London, 1988, p.124.
6. C.S. Lewis, *The Great Divorce*, p.40.

Chapter 6

1. John Bradshaw, *The Family*, Health Communications, Florida, 1988, p.199.
2. Agnes Sanford, *The Healing Light*, Arthur James, Worcs, 1949, p.120.
3. Leanne Payne, *The Healing Presence*, p.64.

Chapter 7

1. Quote from Dr Paul Tournier in: John Powell, *Why Am I Afraid to Tell You Who I Am?*, Argus Comms, Valencia, CA, 1969, p.5.
2. John Powell & Loretta Brady, *Will the Real Me Please Stand Up?*, p.9.
3. Dr Paul Tournier, *A Place For You*, SCM Press, London, 1966, p.16.
4. John Powell & Loretta Brady, *Why Am I Afraid to Tell You Who I Am?*, Tabor Pub., Valencia, CA, 1985, p.12.
5. *Daily Telegraph*, 17.1.90.
6. John Bradshaw, *The Family*, p.50.
7. Charles H. Kraft, *Christianity With Power*, p.33.
8. Dr Paul Tournier, op. cit., p.191.
9. John Powell & Loretta Brady, op. cit., p.18.

Chapter 8

1. Barbara Gordon, *I'm Dancing as Fast as I Can*, p.170.
2. Ibid., p.300.
3. John Powell, *The Secret of Staying in Love*, Tabor Pub., Valencia, CA, 1974, p.100.
4. Ibid., p.103.
5. Ibid., p.104.
6. Richard F. Lovelace, *Dynamics of Spiritual Life*, p.83.
7. Ibid., p.85.
8. Ibid., p.82.
9. Grace Sheppard, *An Aspect of Fear*, p.82.
10. John Powell, *The Christian Vision*, p.16.
11. John Powell, *The Secret of Staying in Love*, p.131.

Chapter 9

1. Barbara Gordon, *I'm Dancing as Fast as I Can*, p.295.
2. John Bradshaw, *The Family*, Health Communications, Florida, 1988, p.2.
3. David Benner, *Psychotherapy and the Spiritual Quest*, p.125.
4. Helena Wilkinson, *Puppet on a String*, Hodder & Stoughton, London, 1984, p.99.
5. Leanne Payne, *The Healing Presence*, p.39.
6. Frank Lake, *Clinical Theology*, p.99.
7. Helena Wilkinson, op. cit., p.183.

Chapter 10

1. Carlo Carretto, *In Search of the Beyond*, Darton, Longman & Todd, London, 1975, p.75.
2. Leanne Payne, *The Healing Prescence*, p.24.
3. Henri J.M. Nouwen, *The Way of the Heart*, Seabury Press, New York, 1981, p.45.
4. Ibid., p.48.
5. Richard Foster, *Celebration of Discipline*, p.85.
6. Ibid., p.86.
7. Barry Kissell, *Walking on Water*, Hodder & Stoughton, London, 1986, p.115.
8. Carlo Carretto, op. cit., p.80.
9. Richard Foster, op. cit., p.168.
10. Leanne Payne, *The Broken Image*, p.139.
11. Grace Sheppard, *An Aspect of Fear*, p.110.
12. Leanne Payne, *The Broken Image*, p.150.
13. Leanne Payne, *The Healing Presence*, p.173.
14. Richard Foster, op. cit., p.9.